THE

UNHEALED

WOUND

· · · · ·

THE CHURCH

AND

HUMAN SEXUALITY

THE

UNHEALED

WOUND

. . . . .

THE CHURCH

AND

HUMAN SEXUALITY

EUGENE KENNEDY

ST. MARTIN'S GRIFFIN ✠ NEW YORK

www.stmartins.com

Library of Congress Cataloging-in-Publication Data

Kennedy, Eugene C.
    The unhealed wound : the Church and human sexuality /
Eugene Kennedy.
        p. cm.
    ISBN 0-312-26637-5 (hc)
    ISBN 0-312-28358-X (pbk)
    1. Sex—Religious aspects—Catholic Church. 2. Celibacy—
Catholic Church. 3. Catholic Church—Doctrines. I. Title.
BX1795.S48 K46 2001
241'.66'08822—dc21   2001018569

First St. Martin's Griffin Edition: March 2002

10 9 8 7 6 5 4 3 2 1

FOR

KITTY BITTERMAN

{1942–1999}

WHOLE, HEALTHY, AND ALWAYS LOVING

&

FOR HER LOVING HUSBAND,

MIKE BITTERMAN

CONTENTS

PART ONE

. . . . .

THE MYTH OF
THE UNHEALED WOUND

OVERTURE: TRISTAN'S WOUND

✝

I T IS THE TWENTY-SECOND day of the last November before the
New Year 2000. A light mist casts a sheen on Manhattan's
streets, veils the Metropolitan Opera House, and blurs the
lights of limousines and taxis delivering guests hungry to see and
hear Richard Wagner's *Tristan und Isolde*. At the end of its first New
York performance 113 years before, according to a newspaper of the
era, "before the clapping (and screaming) began, the audience sat
hypnotized for minutes 'silent and motionless in their places as
though drunk or in a transport.' "[1]

Women "swooned when . . . Tristan tore the bandages from his
wound" to rise from his delirium and greet life again in the return of
Isolde and to die in her arms—as Wagner himself wished to die, in
the embrace of his mistress, Mathilde. The epic *liebesnacht* (the
love night) and the *liebestod* (the love death) were said to "have
shattered inhibitions [of women] inculcated by Gilded Age deco-
rum." With its "erotic maelstrom of . . . love music," one critic
reflects, Wagner's version of the Tristan legend "had changed people's lives."[2]

Do the men and women hurrying toward their places expect
their lives to be changed by what, in 1886, the *New York Tribune*
referred to as the "tumultuous lava current" of the opera? It is less
by chance than by a summons from the millennial, love-straitened
times that Tristan and Isolde are to sing once more of their "love-
death" to New Yorkers who know that in the century just ending, a

sexual revolution has been won but something about love has also been lost. They almost certainly feel within themselves the poisoned wound of Tristan, the gash that lies at the heart of this legend and a dozen kindred myths.

Do these people, so unremarkably human in their desires beneath their designer labels, long for love that is not given by half? And would they, in the fundament of their beings, surrender the right always to choose, and instead be themselves chosen, even imprisoned, by a grand consuming passion and suffer the intense erotic wound of a great love? Are they less sexually restless than the patrons a century earlier, or are they more anxious to meet their Tristan or their Isolde and be swept away by a transcendent love that makes even death sweet?

Enter Wagner's Tristan and enter a myth for the postmodern world, in which the wound symbolizes the still-unhealed division between God and his universe, heaven and earth, and spirit and flesh—that injury that seeds men and women, as Joseph Campbell says, with "longing, irresolution, loneliness and lust."[3] Does the opera intensify fin de siècle ambivalence about the dangerous glory of love that demands a total surrender of the self to another? Do the audience members bear within themselves their own sexual wounds, hoping to tear away their bandages, as Tristan pulls them from his own wound to be healed by, and perhaps to die of, love?

If this is the theme of this titanic psychodrama, Tristan is but one of the great mythical figures who, like all of us, bear a wound that needs healing. Wounds are found everywhere in ancient legends, in those of Sir Gawain and that of the Fisher King, who found ease only in his boat on the water, and in the spell-casting castrate Clinschor, who was himself wounded as he wounded the king. The Grail King in the *Parzival* of von Eschenbach waits for someone to speak the words of healing for a wound so severe that he can neither sit nor stand nor lie down with comfort. The wounds are almost always the same—these great male figures are wounded sexually, by spears thrust through their genitals, and await healing that comes, as we shall see, not from magic or miracles but from responses so simple in their human sympathy or so powerful in their human love that they astound us still.

UNHEALED WOUNDS

✝

I T WAS AN ORDINARY pastoral call by a young priest on an old
lady. At eighty-five, Florence sat straight as a judge and watched
the world through Wedgwood-blue eyes that had missed very
little of what life gave and took away. Florence was a twenty-year
widow after a forty-year marriage and had children and grandchil-
dren unto the third generation. But she could not pronounce the
word *sex*. She managed *sec* hesitantly as she blushed and looked
away.

On such routine visits with people whose names were never in
the papers, I first sensed the throbbing, faint as a tremor far away, of
an unhealed wound.

Tim was seventy-two, a retired history professor turned into Mr.
Chips not by the untimely death of a young wife but by the bache-
lor's existence in which he sought cramped shelter from the torrent
of sexual fantasies that had flooded his imagination since child-
hood. More than sixty years later, he still cringed as he described
the shame heaped on him in his first confessions.

Frank was a few years older, a retired priest-professor who had
achieved acclaim as wide as his life was narrow and proper, and for
a long time he did not appear to be aware of the wound never
healed and never attended to within him. Only long after the battles for commanded chastity had been adjourned had he realized
that he had not won them but instead had fought a strategic
retreat. Now, awkwardly for him and for all who knew him, his

need for closeness surfaced, a touching longing for simple human affection, for all that had been ruled out to keep himself reined in. With half-formed adolescent grace, he would embrace a waitress just a tick too long or hold on, truly for dear life, to women as he greeted them or bade them good night, a good boy who had spent his life on a man's errands, like an orphan finding his true birth record and realizing how little he had known and how late he had loved.

Tom was fifty, a handsome and successful priest on everybody's short list to become a bishop someday. He was looking past me, beyond me, as I walked by him standing in a doorway one night in a West Coast city. He was wearing gold chains over a black turtleneck sweater, his eyes hungry, deprived, searching like those of a thousand men in a thousand urban doorways for a sexual partner. His haunted look has never left me and I knew then as I know better now that he was wounded, too, and that explains the aura of sadness that trailed him until he disappeared from the priesthood, from his bright prospects, too, into a sexual underworld without a forwarding address.

Other faces rise in a long, dazed parade, laypeople and priests, religious men and women, laying down sacks after a long portage; what was is in them anyway? Men and women indicting themselves for their sexual longings, banishing them, themselves, too, into dry and lonely deserts: the hardworking, rosy-cheeked priest whose falling tears sank into the black wool of his cassock as he sobbed of how the need built up in him until, in disguise, he would buy tickets at a big-city ballroom to dance for hours with strangers and, full of remorse, ride in the empty midnight hours the near empty subway home; the pale morning light on the face of a different priest, stunned by death that surprised him in seaman's clothes in a waterfront bar—the woman with him had left, the bartender said.

And I remember the greatly admired bishop who had remained a pastor and heard confessions every week. He had been warned not to raise questions about birth control at bishops' meetings if he wanted to save his ecclesiastical career. His own archbishop had told him, "You'll never become a cardinal that way."

EVERYDAY STIGMATA, EVERYDAY WORLD

In the Gospels, we read often of the multitudes that followed Jesus in search of healing for bleeding, heartbreak, or possession by unclean spirits. Are these crowds of ordinary people struggling to lead good lives all around us any different, really, from those who spread across the hillside listening to Jesus say, "Happy the sorrowing, they shall be comforted"?

Listen to the anguished whispers through the confessional screen of the discouraged bringing their guilt, as lepers brought their sores to Jesus, longing to be cleansed of feelings more often human than sinful; the couples trying to hold love and family together, flailing on the limping carousel of life to keep in touch and keep away from each other during her fertile times; beyond them and beyond counting, good people thinking themselves bad, healthy people thinking themselves sick, ordinary human beings with more than enough other troubles, uncomfortable with their own humanity.

These are not the damned but the saved, gathered at the Last Judgment, surprised that God finds them worthier than they find themselves; these masses overlapping St. Peter's Square and the city and the world beyond are amazed to find that they are garmented in white and that their wounds of being human and sexual are healed at last.

True confessions, all, but few if any sinners to judge here, no purgatory for any of them, either; how could there be eternal penalties for these souls already tortured enough in time? And more sorrow than scandal in these lives that, seen in perspective, are as good and worthy as any. What each suffered was too deep for tears, each from the same unhealed wound branded into them for being human and sexual at the same time.

This is the stigmata suffered by many Catholics, the hidden counterpoint wounds more painful perhaps than the bleeding marks of crucifixion said to be granted to great and famous saints. What wounds are these if not the everyday lacerations of a great multitude of ordinary people, inflicted not by Jesus but often by officials of His Church, as convinced as Salem judges of their righteousness and claiming to speak in His name?

The great uncelebrated good people of the world nurse their own wounds against the background of a culture that, often in bizarre and pathetic ways, is trying to close the wounds in its own sexuality as well. One could pry from the vast curdled coverage of President Bill Clinton's unresolved sexual conflicts one poignant footnote to his own intimate confusion that may in miniature stand for those of the nation. Monica Lewinsky told of Clinton's once keeping a calendar of the days when he was able to control his impulses, the days "when he was good." You can hear America's rueful singing in that phrase, as you can hear it in Marilyn Monroe's childishly sexualized rendition of "Happy Birthday" to President John F. Kennedy as, in the same season, fate rose up around them, as it did also for Ernest Hemingway, each gone down to death with unhealed sexual wounds.

You can read the country's touching stories beneath its noisy bravado and affected sophistication with matters sexual. The covers of *Cosmo* and *GQ* are the shallow veneer on a national uneasiness that remains uncomforted thirty years into the social revolution that promised enlightenment about being sexual and being human at the same time. Neither the world's wound nor, within it, the Church's own related wound has yet been closed. Indiscriminately savoring lust damages people as much as does the reflexive censuring of every erotic impulse.

Bitter on the tongue is the message of the Church, garbled by its dividing nature and spirit, because, deep in its memory and alive still in the Gospel, are healthy appreciations of and attitudes toward both sexuality and sin. This purity of understanding informs

the Catholic Church's primary calling to confirm rather than condemn our humanity, including our pervasive sexuality. Distracted
from or forgetting it, the Church misses entirely the meaning of its
central teaching that God took on our flesh in Jesus, sparing Himself none of our experiences, save sin, in order to heal our wounds
and make us whole.

Jesus' teachings should not send fear into our souls, for he was
always comfortable with sinners and readily forgave those whose
sins seemed to be sexual. I say "seemed" because, as we look more
closely, if the sin is robust enough to be real, the failure, as in adultery, lies in the breach of fidelity and the self-absorption that mur-
ders love and may kill an innocent spouse.

No, the sexual problematic for Catholicism is a function of its
acting as an Institution does rather than as a Church should, so
that its bureaucratic attentions infect what its pastoral possibilities
would otherwise heal. This bureaucracy is a shadow Church that
reflects less the glory of God than the cunning of the world, less a
sense of eternity than of drowning in time. As an institution, its
chief goal is to perpetuate itself—for it is threatened more by time
than by eternity.

This shadow Church keeps itself together as an Institution by
investing its power in keeping its members in a frightened and
dependent state. Wise in the world's ways and friendly with the
Mammon of Iniquity, the Institution knows that if it can control
sexuality, it can maintain its mastery over human beings. This
emphasis on power diminishes its true authority to help ordinary
men and women put away childish things and grow up even by
small steps, the way we learn to walk and talk—the way, imperfect
but tolerant of failings, we become human.

WOUNDED, EVERYONE, EVERYWHERE

✝

POPE JOHN PAUL II BEARS A wound that rises from his own view that Nature and Spirit are enemy camps arrayed against each other in a partitioned country, in a faux barbed-wire peace that barely restrains one from slaughtering the other. In the clerical ascetic imagination, their relationship is ever hostile. Father Scupoli titled his classic account of the soul's purification *The Spiritual Combat*. Throughout this divided tradition, the body is said to "war" against the soul, and Nature is to be "subdued" if not "conquered." Unhealed wounds are the fruit of the kind of chronic guerrilla warfare between Nature and Grace, much as Balkan states battle for reasons older than their claims to the same land, reasons not even the oldest of their old can remember anymore.

Such wars, as in the tinder of the Mideast, Northern Ireland, or the subcontinent, are often struck into flame by the flint of religious differences and often rage for generations, not to achieve victory but to keep the wound from healing. Such conflicts are functions not of religious faith pure and simple but of religious institutions that waste unknowing youth in battles for their vision of human destiny, thereby clothing them in the vesture of myth.

But the bloody tale and its underlying truth of estrangement remains the same everywhere, whether it is Saint Michael battling with Lucifer, Saint Thomas Aquinas hurling an inkpot at the Devil, or, one of many, the missionary in a rainy season at the end of the world pitted against the prostitute in Somerset Maugham's

Rain, Nature and Grace forever raising their lances and charging at each other. The result is often, as it is said, a lost or ruined generation. Nature is destroyed again as, in these sexual sacrifices, generativity is killed in action. For what is taken away, as the war poets tell us, if not the potency of those who will never again feel the sun, know love, or give new life?

Read the headstones at Verdun or in any war cemetery for any side, and find how few were the years granted to these "glorious dead," as they are called. And the Guardian of the Spirit survives as a wounded victor, a Grail King whose potency is also stilled, numbed, diminished, and often steeped in conflict. Inspect the lists of those who have died or been wounded in the battles—supposedly for virtue, or somebody's idea of holiness, into which ecclesiastical generals have committed generations of youth to vindicate their divided image of the human person. There is no burial ground for sexual suffering, no place where it can easily be interred. Sexual suffering must be borne, as every unhealed wound is, by men and women who live with and cannot bury their pain.

CENTURY'S BEGINNING

Listen to the laments from the beginning and the end of the twentieth century, each a plangent cry about sexual woundedness, each about a priest, one real, one fictionalized, but both reflecting aspects of this mythic theme. Indeed, priests are symbolic figures in our examination of the Church and the unhealed wound of human sexuality. For as functionaries of the Institution, they are defined as mediators; so, too, they constitute a medium in which we may read the myth that opens for us an excavation site about the celibate bearer of ecclesiastical sexuality, of the healthy and unhealthy elements of that sexuality, and of the pervasive role that it has played in the emanations of the power and the glory of the Institutional Church.

Our first story is not set in the teeming urban Catholicism of the North that welcomed and prized priests and bishops, but in the Deep South and its patchwork of what were termed "priestless counties." Early in the twentieth century, priests were regarded as barely above blacks in humanity. Not only did they exemplify a foreign religion, they were, like the blacks, a mystery and a threat as well. Like the black man, the priest was the object of a vexing if uncatalogued mythology of sexual possibilities.

Let us listen to the story of Father John Conoley, who served in the 1920s—a period of robust masculine identification for American priests—as Catholic chaplain at the University of Florida at Gainesville. He was popular with the students and well known across the campus and in the city, where he founded the Florida Players, a theatrical group that exists to this day. But to the hardshell locals, he was the representative of not only an alien religion but one characterized in blatant sexual terms as the Whore of Rome, whose rectories and convents were said to be connected by tunnels not of love but of the lust that was the energy for orgies between nuns and priests.

Indeed, Sidney J. Catts, a failed minister and lawyer, ruthlessly exploited anti-Catholicism to gain the governorship of Florida in 1916. It was his brand of bigotry that Father Conoley criticized in a 1917 article in *The Catholic Mind* referring to it as "the deadly original sin of Protestantism" and accusing Catts of "riding into office on promises to . . . eradicate the [Romanism] that was threatening the very life of the Republic."[1]

As Conoley's popularity with the students grew, so did his influence in the city. Both developments irritated the Klansmen, whose white robes often billowed against the Florida night. They set out to get him, as Heloise's uncle set out against Peter Abelard, revealing how threatening his sexuality was to them by spreading rumors about his engaging in sexual relationships with students. The Klan would exact a sexual price in return.

Two of its members, the mayor of the city and its chief of

police, carried out a medieval sentence. Ignorant of how they were taking on mythological roles that we may read clearly at this distance, they kidnapped the priest one February night in 1928, castrated him, and abandoned him on the steps of the Catholic Church in the nearby town of Palatka, a man as broken as Abelard, never to function potently again as priest or man. This is the literal violence that men, frightened of their own sexual impulses, commit against other men whose actions and success reveal an unselfconscious potency that so intimidates the former that, in order to save themselves, they must destroy them.

PRIEST GENDER AND CATHOLIC EXPERIENCE

The priest of the first half of the twentieth century, intelligent if not intellectual, seemed to reflect what Americans in general expected at that time in men, a steady if underplayed masculinity, prized for the sureness of their self-control; and if they did not advertise their emotions, neither did they seem in need of the proof texts of Hemingway-like adventures. In the social index of the movies that flourished in the latter scenes of this period, priests were typically portrayed by actors of such undeniable masculine presence as Spencer Tracy or Charles Bickford. The manly priest's celibacy added sex to the drama and romantic mystery to his own person.

In the priest as a sexual persona we find a readable text about American Catholicism and about Catholicism in general. This subject has seldom been explored; indeed, it has often been marked as off-limits for questions of any kind. In the sex and gender identification of priests—in what we may call, in a wide context of meanings, the sexual experience of priests—we uncover the strata that run like rivers with stories of other times and of our own times.

Throughout this period, the priest stands in splendid ecclesiastical grandeur as a holy man who follows in the footsteps of Jesus.

He enjoys a calling that sets him apart from but also above other Catholics. Still, he is never separate from his shadow self, that subtler, not wholly secret self, as psychiatrist Carl Jung describes it, in which another side of personality, of fainter qualities and graver possibilities, can be found. That is the human penumbra falling from the once divinized figure of the priest. Priests, in company with all of us, catch fleeting glimpses of this other, alien self.

SEXUAL SUBTEXTS

During the drama that lasted from Vatican I (1869–70) almost to Vatican II (1962–65), the priest was perceived as possessing intriguing, if not vexing, theatrical potential. The period's mythmakers, lesser and greater, recognized the powerful mythic potential of the Arthurian knight in these men who remained virile and sexual beneath the armor of their chaste celibacy. This seemed no distant and abstract choice by a man beyond temptation, but a sacrifice of love, companionship, and sexuality whose banked energies could burst into flame at any moment.

Henry James employs the theme of the man caught between love of the Church and love of a woman and his posterity in his 1895 play, *Guy Domville*. Graham Greene explores the survival of the sacred even in the fallen "whisky priest" hero of his 1938 novel, *The Power and the Glory*. The American priest is a romantic but secure celibate in the popular 1944 movie *Going My Way*, in which Father O'Malley's choice of the Church over his old girlfriend, now an opera star, is nonetheless that of a real man in relationship to a real woman. This priest is an unambivalent sexual being who weds the Church instead of the beautiful woman. It is the underlying reality of his masculinity that makes the priest believable in this slight screenplay. The sexual subtext is heavily charged in the scenes between priest Bing Crosby and nun Ingrid Bergman in the 1945 sequel, *The Bells of St. Mary's*.

The priest appears in the popular culture of the period as no less sexual for having sacrificed its expression in marriage. He is portrayed as having integrated his sexuality into his well-controlled manliness. Ministers, although married, seldom walk across the screen in the same forceful way. They are good men, as Fredric March shows in 1941's *One Foot in Heaven*, but they lack sexual mystery. It is, we suggest, that sense of sexuality mastered but not denied to which directors responded by casting strong actors to portray priests. That reciprocal tension between sexually potent actors and sexually controlled priests gives depth and texture to Spencer Tracy's Father Flanagan in the 1938 *Boys Town* and Pat O'Brien's Father Duffy in 1940's *The Fighting 69th*; Gregory Peck's China missionary, Father Francis Chisholm, in 1944's *The Keys of the Kingdom*; and, perhaps, at the very end of that period, to Karl Malden's priest among brawling longshoremen in 1954's *On the Waterfront*.

These entertainments reflect what the priest symbolized during the larger drama of Church life between the two Vatican councils. This was the priest rooted in the Brick and Mortar era, the down-to-earth boy from the neighborhood called to a higher state, the priest who might otherwise have been a major leaguer, whose male identity seemed certain and yet undeniably seasoned by sexuality. Such a priest is an intrinsically romantic figure, for he seems to be in command of sexual impulses that bedevil the best of other men. He is the strong but gentle man idealized during the early period of the women's movement.

CENTURY'S END

In strange, almost apocalyptic symmetry, the 1999 television season began with our second story from the CBS hospital drama *Chicago Hope*. In its first episode we encounter, transformed, the same myth once more. The century had witnessed it many times, for example, in novels that took the pulse of the age such as in Hemingway's *The Sun Also Rises*, with its sexually wounded hero, Jake Barnes. A priest has his penis bitten off; "frantic," as the CBS *Episode Guide* tells us, "to keep his injury confidential," he comes to the emergency room, "fearing bad publicity for himself and his church."

How differently the sexual celibate is perceived at century's end than at its beginning. How does the *Chicago Hope* priest differ from Father Conoley? He is not seen as a threatening man of potency but as vulnerable, somehow weakened, inviting a wounding.

In the great myths of the twentieth century, totalitarianism emasculates the male figure through the wars and violent repression that are the institutional agencies of maintaining control. Hemingway originally planned that the wound inflicted by World War I on Jake Barnes would leave him with a sexual appetite and no penis, utterly tragic because he cannot be healed and cannot express his love for a woman. Emasculation, profound but irreparable sexual wounding, is the product of totalitarian institutions, whether of Church or State. Thus, the brutality of the Soviet Union is revealed as the sexual capacity of the protagonist in Solzhenitsyn's *The Cancer Ward* is destroyed by state-sponsored radiation and chemotherapy.

The CBS television program repeats the myth unknowingly, unconsciously symbolizing the enormous social changes that have taken place in the world and the Church—and how the issues of the decade and of the century, of sex and violence, of sensation's devouring of narrative, of belief and mystery, of chaos and order, as well as of potency and manhood, are flares drawing our attention in surreal fashion to the estrangement of Nature and Spirit. They are attached to a priesthood that rides into the wilderness as a scapegoat bearing the sins of the Church that, as Institution, is kin to every other institution in its pursuit of control through instinctive attacks on sexual potency. The television plot is a shadow creation compared with those of Hemingway and Solzhenitsyn, as it is a shadow re-enactment of the 1928 Florida event, a revelation in pale tones of damaged manhood and capacity destroyed, a blurred fragment of a larger truth about the institutional Church, that Guardian of the Spirit sexually wounded by its battle with Nature.

STRONG MEN NO MORE

The comic-relief priest of the M*A*S*H series a generation before was only an agent of transition in the public cultural judgment of the priest and, therefore, of the Institutional Church. In the HBO television series *The Sopranos*, the priest is portrayed as the already emasculated sybarite who settles for a spiritualized sensuality, consumed with recipes and film stars, as he comes to be fed and to watch DVDs with the wife of the Mafia leader. In the final episode, she sends him away, stunning him in her brutally frank reading of his manhood, "You only want the whiff of sexuality."

Here, then, is the American priest, less a threatening sexual persona to be dealt with than an asexual creature whose wound was inflicted long ago in the shadow side of the Church, by power exercised with primitive reflexes by men out to control other men. This wound remains unhealed. Indeed, the priest figure, save for the ABC series *Nothing Sacred*, canceled the year before for lack of viewers, is a man not yet a man, to be pitied for his lack of development, a man perceived as having diminished manhood.

The priest thus portrayed is not the priest many people know and admire. Yet this weakened character has not entered the mythological field by accident or without cause. Is he a prophet of a future priesthood and of the way sexuality will be dealt with by seminarians who seem self-absorbed, if not fey, in proclaiming their plan to bring birth control and masturbation back as subjects to preach against from their pulpits?[2]

The crisis of priest pedophilia that exploded in the mideighties revealed that the sexual wound in the American priesthood remained unhealed but no longer concealed. Before a stunned nation, the priest was paraded—behold the sexually immature child abuser, a man ruined and shamed. Still unexplored, much less acknowledged, by ecclesiastical officials is that the tragic emasculation was not the work of bigoted outsiders, as it had been with Father Conoley long ago in Gainesville, Florida, but that of insiders with a similar need to control heterosexuality.

The broken and stunted sexuality of many priests led to public humiliation as searing as that experienced by Oscar Wilde after his conviction for sodomy at the end of the nineteenth century. Scores of cases of pedophilia have been uncovered, and like the debtor in the Gospel parable, the priest has been handed over to the jailer until he pays what he owes. The priest is the wounded mythic figure, the wounded seeker of the Grail, Sir Gawain; Abelard groaning across the centuries from the attack of other men; and Anfortas, whose infection and pain arise from that deep and unattended estrangement in the spiritual institution—the Church from this world, Spirit from Nature, the terrible price of a divided image of personality.

For this old estrangement, whose symptoms are now revealed in the Institutional priesthood, reflects the drama of the Scholasticism of which Abelard was a pioneer master teacher but which in his time was greatly feared and finally broken by this official Church. As Joseph Campbell puts it, "The fate of its initiator, Abelard—the Waste Land theme of the agony of his life—had been the announcement, as in a symphony, of all the passages to follow . . . [of] the same dreadful murder of light and life by grim power (the art of the systematic exercise of power by men over men) was to be rehearsed."[3]

A NEW MYTHOLOGY

The respect and social support given to such priests by their parishioners throughout the then cohesive Catholic culture strongly reinforced them and their "special" character. This also obscured the shadow self of the priesthood that, if occasionally seen in the tyrannical pastor or the alcoholic curate, was quickly washed out by the favorable and forgiving light in which they were viewed. Only as the century deepened and, for a number of reasons, the fragmenting Catholic culture melded into the general American culture did this silhouette detach itself and reveal the layered complexity of its darkness. This, too, has been chronicled in stories and myths from this side of the century. In them we discover the priest as a figure who lives out a sexually charged myth that we have not previously examined clearly about him and the Church as an Institution.

4

THE MYTH OF THE
GRAIL KING ANFORTAS

✝

The King fared forth alone that day (which was to prove a sorrow to his people), riding in quest of adventure, steered along by his joy in love: for love's zeal so compelled him. And he was pierced, wounded in a joust, by a poisoned spear through his testicles, so severely he could not be healed.

A heathen it was who had there engaged him and delivered that stroke: one born in the land of Ethnise, where the river Tigris flows from Paradise: one who had been confident that his battle courage would gain the Grail for him. Its name was engraved on his heathen spear, and in quest of knightly deeds afar, he was wandering over land and sea, only for the power of the Grail.

The heathen was there slain by the King; and for him too we may somewhat lament. However, when the King returned to us so pale and empty of strength, a doctor's hand searched the wound, found the spearhead therein, a splinter of the shaft as well, and removed them. . . . Whereupon, he was immediately borne through God's help, to the Grail: but when he looked upon it his torture only increased, for he was now unable to die.[1]

—WOLFRAM VON ESCHENBACH, *PARZIVAL*

THIS LEGEND, AS JOSEPH Campbell explains, reveals how shattering the unity of human personality—setting flesh at odds with spirit, mind with body, and creation against Creator—always follows from slaying Nature, that is, what is natural and healthy in us, in pursuit of a Grail of what we might term unnatural, or inhuman, spiritual perfection:

> The young king's name, Anfortas, from the old French Enfertez (Enfermetez), means "Infirmity." Its prophecy is fulfilled . . . when the two riders collide, to the ruin of both. Nature is then dispatched, and the guardian of the symbol of the spirit, though emptied of his virtue, is nevertheless retained by his sorrowing people, ever in hope of healing, but without event.
>
> The life-desolating effects of this separation of nature (the Earthly Paradise) and the spirit (the Castle of the Grail) in such a way that neither touches the other but destructively, remains to this day an essential psychological problem of the Christianized Western world. . . . Since it is at its root a consequence of . . . an ontological distinction between God and his universe, creator and creature, spirit and matter, it is a problem that has hardly altered since it first became intolerably evident at the climax of the Middle Ages."[2]

THE MYTH OF PARZIVAL

In von Eschenbach's *Parzival*, the young knight sets out through many adventures to find and heal the suffering Grail King. On first entering the king's presence, however, Parzival is so focused on himself and so constrained by court protocol—itself driven by ambition that prefers silence to words that might offend the king— that he fails to speak what is in his heart, and the Grail King remains in his agony. Cursed for his failure, Parzival is exiled to the wilderness, where he passes through a crisis of belief. He rejects "what he took to be God," the distant, demanding Lord of such superficial court dictates, and experiences "a deep break in the spiritual life . . . as a necessary prelude to his healing of the Maimed King."[3] Parzival may be said to pass through the transformation described centuries later by psychologist Gordon Allport as *extrinsic*, from belief in the externals because somebody urges you, to *intrinsic* faith, belief tested by crisis, internalized and made your own.[4]

The catalyst for this deepening of faith is Parzival's awakening, through the experience of true heterosexual love in his meeting with Condwiramurs, so that he grasps "a new ideal of love (*amor*) as the sole motive for marriage and an indissoluble marriage as the sacrament of love."[5] Thus matured, Parzival, "because of this love marriage and through his loyalty to the sacrament . . . was to achieve at last the healing of Anfortas and succeed to the throne *without* inheriting his wound."[6]

This spiritual insight into faithful love enables Parzival to overcome the social pressures, as we might say, of the official Church, whose bookkeeper God he puts aside along with the rule-obsessed court bureaucracy, to ask the question, as simple and profoundly human as it is free of every external trick and manipulation, the inquiry from his heart that heals. He asks the sexually wounded king—and would heal us, too—"What is it that ails you?"

What prevailing attitude does Parzival overcome if not the distortion of the love that makes us whole into an external and dehumanized sacrament "held as far as possible apart from the influence of *amor*, to be governed only by the concerns of security and reputation, politics and economics: while love, known as *eros*, was to be sublimated as *agape*, and if any such physical contact occurred as would not become a monk or a nun, it was to be undertaken dutifully, as far as possible without pleasure, for God's purpose of repopulating those vacant seats in Heaven which had been emptied when the wicked angels fell."[7]

Myth is the true voice of men and women in which they speak

of—and save against time, chance, and death—everything that is
spiritually true about themselves. Myth is, therefore, the language
of the scriptures and all writings about the ways of the soul, and of
the ways of the body, too, if we understand that body and soul cannot be sundered without desperately wounding the personality they
constitute.

That is the meaning of the myth of the Grail King Anfortas:
when, for whatever hope or creed, we slay Nature, that is, everything that is natural and healthy about us, including our sexuality,
we injure ourselves grievously, inflicting a wound that, remembered
in many legends, is always sexual. In slaying Nature, as many strive
mightily to do in seeking the illusory Grail of spiritual perfection,
by divinizing the spirit and demonizing the body, we not only
wound ourselves sexually but salt the wound so that it does not easily heal. The French say that the person "who tries to be an angel
ends up a beast." It is just another way of describing how we commit sacrilege against ourselves when, in the name of whatever
extrinsic spiritual ambition, we plunder, by force or fasting, the
wholeness of human personality.

This is the guiding myth for our reflections on how much harm
has been done to Nature (that which is natural, and therefore not
evil, about us) through the institutionalization of the tragic disfig-
urement of the human person by the Church—as an Institution
ever and always distinguished from the Church as Mystery—whenever it defines itself over against creation, or the world, whenever,
in the name of a false and inhuman spirituality, it slays Nature and
so lacerates anew its old sexual wound. We explore these wounds
because our guiding myth, that is, our spiritual story, also tells us
how this wound may be healed, how the Grail King, so aggrieved
that he can neither stand nor sit nor lie down, may, in fact, be made
whole again.

In the myth of Parzival we learn how simply this healing takes
place and how easily such healing is within the grasp of the Church
as an Institution that suffers so much now, passing its pain on to

ordinary men and women. For Parzival's question to the sexually wounded king lacks mystery as it expresses all Mystery, "What is it that ails you?"

BLESSED POPE JOHN XXIII

The inquiry cuts through the falsified atmosphere of the court as, we might say, centuries later Pope John XXIII cut across the false protocol of a bureaucratic Church by, in effect, asking the same question of the world. He did not thunder about the world's evil, he did not condemn or ask for repentance in sackcloth and ashes. Rather, he felt sorrow for the world's sadness and, from his own pastor's heart, asked Parzival's question, *the* question that dissolved age-old enmities so that Protestant Belfast would toll its bells in mourning when he died.

Blessed Pope John not only placed the question himself but called the Church into general council to reform itself pastorally so that it could place the healing question to the world from which it had separated itself for so long. The council returned the Church to its understanding of itself as Mystery rather than just Institution, to a deepened profession of intrinsic rather than just extrinsic faith. Our meditations lead us back to that same disposition toward human beings. It is within the pastoral tradition of the Church to subordinate its official, protocol-ridden self to its singular calling as Mystery, so that, aware of its own wounds, it may ask this question as it embraces its wounded flock, "What is it that ails you?"

5

JOHN PAUL II, WOUNDED HEALER

✝

WE MAY LOOK AGAIN now at Pope John Paul II and read more deeply the mythical significance of his more than a hundred journeys throughout the world. On the surface of headlines and instant history, they are the great confessional pilgrimages of a contemporary pope who has made himself master of modern invention in order to preach the Gospel to the earth's far corners and, at the same time, dominate the imagination of his own Church.

Some mythic figures are locked into an unresolved destiny so that Sisyphus's exertions never end, Atlas cannot shrug free of the world, and Rachel weeps forever for her children. John Paul II shares this mythic isolation, this unrelieved calling. At their mythic, spiritual level, the Pope's pilgrimages dissolve, the seemingly separate trips melding into one so that each is the same journey, taken up again and never ended, each an aspect of an extraordinary and painful spiritual odyssey. Although the Pope's travels seem as triumphant as Jesus' passage through the gates of Jerusalem to the hosannas of the Palm Sunday crowd, they are more the stark and staggering bearing of the crossbar through the shouts that rain down like blows on the way to Calvary.

How otherwise can the Pope appear such a burdened man as he pursues his quest, ever that of Good Friday, his head bent low, as Jesus' must have been, so that he sees the stones of harsh reality, always the same sorrowful stones, of the Via Dolorosa, toward a crucifixion that never takes place, so that he seems never freed from this mystical calling, from being the wounded healer who can never say, "It is finished"?

Pope John Paul II, son of both the East and the West, seems ever just short of his goals because, as some scholars argue of Jesus, his consciousness of his mission comes only slowly and he does not fully grasp why he is condemned to make but never complete the Stations of the Cross before the world. Pilate wears a different face at every airport as he turns him over to the crowd, and the women of Jerusalem are now brown and now black and others are almond eyed, and the Pope finds his image taken away by photographers, as Jesus' was in legend on Veronica's cloth. He stumbles and falls before the pilgrims in his Roman audience hall, sensing even more than when he was shot a dozen years before the losses he has suffered and the sure narrowing of the way before him. Yes, he says, he will drink of this cup; has he not seen his own body contract into chalky whiteness from the stripes he has borne? What is this mystery in which I am wounded but cannot yield up my spirit to the Father?

Mythically and mystically, Pope John Paul II's calling is to transcend cultural differences, to reveal to humankind that it is one family, and to harken to the theme of unity in a divided world. Yet he seems torn asunder by his efforts to unify, a man perhaps more of sorrows than of joy, troubled by, yet sure of, his messianic role. If he has prayed with Paul that he might be emptied, he still clings dutifully to the monarchical glories of his office. If in his prime as a bold and confident leader, he stood before the White House to shame a thousand Baptist apocalyptic visions of such an event, he has been girded in his old age, as his predecessor Peter was, to "be led in a way" that he "would rather not go."

HIERARCHICAL CROSS, MYTHICAL WOUND

What is this invisible cross that John Paul bears across the continents? Do his narrowed eyes, searching ever beyond the faces of those to whom he speaks, tell us that he looks constantly for the Golgotha on which he can finally die? Or does he communicate something else to us—something other, surely, than happiness and something unconnected with and unexpressed by majesty? In the dimension of myth, he is the wounded Grail King who can find no place of comfort, much less relief, nowhere that he can sit or stand or lie. Like the Fisher King, it is only as he is transported away from his castle, only in flashing moments in another medium, in the air rather than on the water, that he is briefly the fisher of men.

And prisoner he is to this pain, as the Grail King was, because as the law of the latter's court forbade the knights from speaking healing human truths to him, so the rules of the papal court enforce silence on any who could speak truths that might at least cast light on why he cannot finish the course and be relieved of his suffering. And yet he is master of who may speak and what they may say, for a few years into his pontificate, he set down rules for the Roman synods of the world's bishops that reserved all subjects for discussion and all resolutions solely to himself.

The Pope's unseen mythical cross is heavy with history, for John Paul, so much otherwise a man of this age, has borne the weight of another age to the millennium. Unlike the sealed door of St. Peter's that fell open at his word for the Jubilee celebration, the portal to the twenty-first century, like the Gospel's narrow gate, allows no space for the passage of this cross. John Paul carries the cross of hierarchical structure, of the monarchical model of the Church and the papacy, whose wood warps and splits and whose rough grain does not match the smooth wholeness of the unity of human experience being rediscovered in the Space Age.

Indeed, this extraordinary pope carries in himself the conflict, misreading it as deliverance, his vision divided as, on the one hand, he sees the great Christian Mystery at the center of all history while, on the other, he perceives its life as essentially linked to and dependent on accidental hierarchical forms that have been scattered by the centrifugal winds of that same history. John Paul II doggedly bears the cross of literalism and institutionality that he strives to raise, with the aid of eager Simons of Cyrene, as the sign in which Catholicism will conquer in the twenty-first century.

But this vision, like a flawed notion of the Grail, emphasizes the accidents of structure over the essentials of Mystery, making the Church again into an Institution rather than Vatican II's People of God, and replacing *collegiality* with *communio*, a pre-Copernican ordering of the ecclesiastical cosmos in which the Pope is the sun and the bishops are but pale moons that reflect his light.

Patron of science and astronomers, restorer of Galileo's reputation, visitor to the Wailing Wall in Jerusalem to heal the rift between the Church and the Jewish people, this pope follows a different course within the Church, exhausting himself by attempting to force an outdated model of reality onto human experience, including the sexual, in which he emphasizes the very division that he struggles to end. He urges unquestioning conformity as a greater value than unity and freedom of the spirit. He has sadly been wounded himself in this effort, not with the nail prints of Jesus but with the eternal mythical wound that robs him of rest and of which he cannot be cured and of which he cannot die. John Paul's public agony is uncomforted because it is a function of the draining burden of the Church as stones and laws rather than of the life begetting suffering of the Church as Mystery.

Many years from now, it will be easier to see how powerfully the physical wounds of John Paul's papacy have symbolized his mythical wounds: for example, his being shot by a man who rode out of the East into the crowd before St. Peter's, much as the Heathen Knight charged from that same East to do fateful battle with the Guardian of the Spirit in the West; or, again before crowds in his Vatican audience hall, the Pope's tripping on the hem of his own garment, on that symbol of his office, that hem that on Jesus' garment people sought to touch, and the bloodied garment like that over which the soldiers rolled dice. Like Tristan, John Paul bears a wound deep in his thigh that diminishes his powers even as he pulls away the bandages to fill the stage with his presence, overwhelmed with longing, singing to the world of both love and death.

THE SPEAR TIP

Pope John Paul II is ever restless because his wound is a result of thinking one way about persons as sexual beings and acting in a quite different way when dealing with them. The misery and mystery of his papacy are entwined with this hierarchical model of both cosmos and personality. This pattern of the universe was first drawn in what is now Iraq in that same valley of the Euphrates from which that Heathen Knight rode to his death at the sword of the Grail King. This ancient myth reveals the meaning of the present papal struggle and torture. In that encounter, we recall, the West's Grail King and Guardian of the Spirit was himself wounded in his manhood by the Eastern knight he killed. From that injury the spear tip of the rider from the East was later extracted.

The spear tip that infects the wound of the Western spirit is the riven model of the universe devised by the Sumerian priests of the East. Observing the passage of planets through fixed stars four thousand years before the birth of Christ, they imagined the universe as divided and mapped with heaven above and the earth below. This decisive split image was imposed, as if it were their natural structure, on kingdoms and cultures and on human personality as well. From this view arose astrology based on the gods hanging their lanterns in their heavenly houses and the effort, found still in the morning paper, to associate earthly events with scenarios in the stars. From this same source in the sky came the idea that God had embossed His seal on the hierarchical ordering of all reality.

This was the accepted notion, endorsed as an article of faith by the Council of Trent, so that whoever disagreed with this reality as it was reflected in a divinely established hierarchical Church might be declared anathema. This Eastern construct justified a hierarchical Church arrayed like an earthly kingdom with a pope with court and courtiers and the divine right to rule over people distributed in descending tiers to the bottom rank of the ordinary lay folk. This organization of the universe was rejected by Galileo and Copernicus, who were condemned by the Church for the purity and genius of their insight. As the theory of the flat earth died with the first great sea voyages on which men came upon fresh horizons every morning, so the division between the earth and heavens was healed by the first space voyages that discovered that there was no *up* and no *down;* neither were there horizons in a universe centered on the sun and cloaked in the mystery of its unbroken unity.

SEXUAL CONSEQUENCES

If the false notion of a divided universe justified such humanly crippling outcomes as the caste system and slavery, it also rationalized the hierarchical organization of Christendom and, within that, a disastrous structuring of human personality. John Paul II advertises this division in himself in countless ways, perhaps most obviously in the startling difference between his views of the person as a philosopher and his outlook on the person as a pope. Theoretically, he understands and defends the unity of personality, even in his writings on human love and sexuality. How is it that this brilliant leader casts all this aside in his theological practice, to view men and women as divided against themselves, spirit warring against the flesh, chastity ranked above marriage, and the Church ever and always right in judging sexuality because, in the argument that admits of no discussion, much less dissent, the Church as Institution can never make a mistake?

It is understandable that we might view John Paul II as the great tragic figure of our time because his abstractions, reflecting his own wound, in turn wound others when they are applied to flesh-and-blood human beings. One can applaud all the good that he has done and yet feel keenly for his distress as he is undone before the world by this wound that he has never been able to identify correctly. He may feel and yet misread its symptoms, for they are, in a true sense, sexually frustrating for him. How painful and yet how puzzling for the Pope that the more he insists on certain teachings and the more he attaches his personal imprint to them—as in ordering Joseph Cardinal Ratzinger, prefect of the Congregation for the Doctrine of the Faith, to declare as infallible the papal assertion that the Church cannot ordain women—the more he experiences his impotence, his frustrated ability to father a teaching of compelling inner authority.

The Pope has also revealed his spiritual kinship to star-crossed kings in an autocratic style that matches those of all-powerful monarchs from other times. If he fought bravely and effectively to raise the Iron Curtain of communism, he has lowered another across the Institutional Church, which he has attempted to rule as an unreconstructed monarch. But this style, through which he deals with the Church as a hierarchical institution rather than as Mystery incarnated in a People of God, reveals his woundedness.

How are we to understand, rather than misunderstand out of misconceived loyalty, the authoritarian manner in which John Paul, out of his own intimate woundedness, has wounded (or allowed subordinates to wound) humans in ways that are profoundly sexual? This sexual element is never attributed to the actions of the Church as Institution or of the leader of that Institution, and yet they are here clearly present, are hardly subtle, and are not hard to read. Indeed, Pope John Paul II re-enacts the myth of the Grail King before our eyes. How, by any measure of conscience, can we deny it or refuse to examine it?

For what prevents the Pope from recognizing the nature of his own plaguing woundedness if not that which impedes its healing, the court protocol and insubstantial propriety that, in the case of the Grail King, forbade anybody from asking an understanding human question and, in the case of the papal court, demands silence, a muteness that neuters everyone who might speak the word and so bring him wholeness?

The tragedy of the Grail King lies, of course, first in his wound, sustained in his sexual organs in the battle in which Grace gains an illusory triumph over Nature. For, as what is of Nature is slain, so an emptiness overtakes the surviving but separated Spirit that is now sexually restive, sexually damaged, sexually impotent because humanly no longer whole—in short, the contemporary West and the guardian of its spiritual tradition, the papacy, the sexual wound a crimson seam that runs through them all.

We may, then, ride with Parzival, who in von Eschenbach's version is not so different from us. For he is not of a royal line and must therefore prove himself as he quests, as indeed we all do, for the castle of the Grail King, who, because of his sexual wound, can find no comfort or ease and is caught in a never-ending time out of time. If he cannot be cured by either incantation or sacrifice, he may yet be, as may we all, by asking a simple human question about this unhealed wound. Our Grail King is the Pope, his castle the vast conforming Vatican in which his anguish continues because within its walls it is so hard to ask the simple questions that may heal and save us.

6

OUR MYTH,
OUR EXPERIENCE, OUR STORY

✝

BEFORE GOING FURTHER, WE may reflect briefly on some of the terms that we have already encountered and others that invite our understanding. Our guiding legend or myth concerns the sexually wounded Grail King, a tale told in many ways across the centuries. If it is steeped in sacramental significance in von Eschenbach's telling, it is stripped of this in Wagner's *Tristan*. Yet the elements of the underlying story remain the same.

The idea of myth as a "fiction" or "false belief," as in George Washington's long-ago truthfulness about the chopped-down cherry tree or today's urban legends, has long clouded its fundamental meaning, which is transparent in the Greek *mythos* (story). Myth refers to our human story, the tale of the family we all belong to, as it has been told with different inflections in different cultures, throughout history.

A story is the only secure line on which to transmit the defining truths about our human nature. We hear the story of poll-doomed Harry Truman's underdog victory over Thomas E. Dewey in the 1948 presidential election, but it is a tale many times told, going back to and even beyond David and Goliath. We never get enough of it, as a whole series of *Rocky* movies attest, for it is a narrative of a deep and lasting truth. Audiences never weary of *Casablanca*, not because it is a story of war but because it is a chronicle of romantic love. That movie has become a *myth* about men and women, love and sacrifice and the risk of death, the same story found in the Arthurian legends. Or, as Joseph Campbell puts it, "the latest version of *Beauty and the Beast* is taking place right now at a bus stop at Fifth Avenue and Forty-second Street." Spiritually, we all live east of Eden now, and memories of innocence and exile resonate just beneath the clatter of the everyday, deep within us.

That is why story, rather than literal history, is the language of religion, why Jesus spoke in parables whose characters still surround us: the complacent boasting of their generosity in churches and temples, the timid burying their gifts in the ground out of fear of putting them at risk, ordinary people beating their breasts and murmuring of their sinfulness, good Samaritans nursing the fallen, greedy men counting their gold before dying that night, good thieves entering Paradise, and widows with no more than a mite to give away. Their stories are in this morning's newspapers.

Myth, then, is the durable form of our spiritual stories, and as scripture scholar John L. McKenzie explains, the "reality which myth presents in symbolic form is the unknown transcendental reality which lies beyond observation and simple deduction, but which is recognized as existing and operative. This reality is perceived and represented in events and not abstraction, and the event is portrayed in the form of a story."[1] The tension in our lives, the shock of recognizing our plight in long-ago stories, arises from living together a myth of religious mystery. The principal work of the Church is to tend this mystery and its symbols.

Our mythic adventure finds us facing trials endured throughout history by those seeking spiritual growth and wisdom. We are now living in the greatest transformation of religious awareness since the Reformation. Everything is at stake for Roman Catholics—and structurally as well as spiritually for the Institutional Church—because, encompassing and transcending all its reforms, the Second Vatican Council (1962–65) reopened the doors of its own long-shuttered storehouse of spiritual myth. Vatican II was, and is, an "event" breaking us out of time, rather than an "episode" that, like a storm or revolution, stirs the world for a moment, then passes as its energies wane.

Through the dynamic mythic event of Vatican II, the Church began to examine the wounds that it sustained, as did the Grail King, in slaying Nature by separating Creator and creation, defining itself over against the world, and opening a rift between intellect and emotion as well as body and spirit from which it has not yet recovered. Nor have we. The Church lives in anguish because its wound is unhealed, as is the wound it transferred to the universe.

This seeping wound is sexual, as all the wounds of mythic figures are. The Institutional Church continues to look past its own wound as it seeks to maintain the painful division that it imposes on human experience. One need only examine briefly the major issues that, with an intensity belying any claim to confidence, the Institutional Church proposes and defends as if they were the eternal dogmatic foundations of its existence: birth control; the celibate priesthood; the control of women and their exclusion from the priesthood; the identification of homosexuality as an "objective disorder" that begets evil; and even, as we shall see, the sexual wound at the root of what it terms the "vocation crisis"—the dynamic of emasculation from which the Church draws energy to punish and to control, its own barely admitted and still largely unexamined crisis of sexual conflicts, evidenced in thousands of cases of priest pedophilia.

These are signs, as clear as one could find, of the unhealed wound of sexuality within institutional Catholicism, which, with guidance from the myths that cast light in our own darkness, we will examine in this book.

NATURE: SEX AND PERSONALITY

We speak of Nature not as some great impersonal personification of forces outside us—Mother Nature, or nature, red in tooth and claw—but as that from which we are generated, that creation of which we are the fruit. The word *nature* may be traced back from the Latin *nasci* (to be born) through the family of concepts in which we discover—whether in the Old English *kin* or *kind* (family); the Germanic *kundjaz*, which means the same; the later German *kind*, as in *kinder* (children); the Latin *genus* and its cluster of *gender* and *generate*; or the Greek *genos* and *genea* (again, race and family)—that, as with the glinting veins of the gold in the passage, our origins, our common inheritance, our calling to generate, to beget, to be sexual and generative, are unmistakably symbolized.

Of Nature, then, we are, in psychiatrist Harry Stack Sullivan's words, "much more simply human than anything else." We focus on the human person, whose life, dignity, and meaning stand at the center of Catholic commitment and concern. The person who acts, to use one of Pope John Paul II's concepts, is not just a mind or a body and is certainly not the caricature of personhood that underlay distinctions, made routinely in moral theology manuals before Vatican II, between the "higher" and "lower" faculties, between the "more noble" and "less noble" parts of the body. Recovering a sense of the unity of personality requires our getting rid of fig leaves and viewing it whole, as spirit and flesh, as mind and body, as gender and sex, without downplaying or emphasizing one aspect over the other in ways that distort or damage the whole.

Vatican II's clear, if exceedingly difficult, commitment was to scale away the wild growth of ideation and imagery that had all but obscured this remarkable unity. Confident presuppositions about men and women that had been employed for centuries demanded sensitive inspection in light of rapid advances in scientific, theological, and scriptural disciplines. Men and women could be understood only if one understood and freely examined the complexities of gender, that genetic manifest and template for the masculine and feminine—and the layers of their sexuality—that fusing of carnality and spirituality that dominates our awareness in its explicit expression even as, in fainter but nonetheless true ways, it manifests itself in every human activity.

SEXUALITY AND CREATIVITY

Creativity is a bundle of gifts, and its energy is a compound rather than a single basic element. Sexuality, adverted to or not, is found in that intense summation and deployment of human energies that we term *creativity*. Indeed, the creative process ignites erotic sparks as it possesses and expresses the fully engaged person. Everything created possesses a sexual component, each creation expressing, as fully as a fingerprint, the unique identity of its creator. Sexuality is integrated into the work that comes from within the creator to live a life of its own as a new creation. This is obvious in the birth of a child but is equally true in a wide range of human authorship, as in a book, a symphony, a ballet, or, as great saints tell us, in scaling the Everest of the spirit in the long dark night's journey into mystical prayer. How else could we react except totally, humanly, to such an extraordinary transport of the complete self? So, too, we must not be surprised to find sexuality expressed in a well-taught course, a wholehearted ministry, a deep friendship—in short, in every aspect of a well if imperfectly lived life.

Sexuality—the sign and energy of male and female—is necessarily present in every creative overture or undertaking. If it is necessarily present in humanity's love, it is undeniably present in humanity's work as well. Should integration of its elements fail, the result is pornography, whether in love debased by manipulation, a truth made shallow in a novel, or the human image ill drawn in an encyclical. Such outcomes betray their creators just as they diminish their creation.

Whenever we author something from within ourselves, whenever we draw on our capacity for generativity, whenever we respond in a human relationship, we act as sexual persons. We are forever creating and re-creating ourselves, one another, and our world. Being human is ever and always profoundly sexual. It is more like life—untidy, imperfect, tasting of joy and sorrow—than still life, whose blossoms never fade and whose fruit never ripens.

SEXUAL SUFFERING

The official Church's persistent misunderstanding of, or failure to follow, the healthy pastoral instincts of, the Church as Mystery about human sexuality is documented more in the pain and discomfort of the nameless millions than in the public repudiation of those scholars and pastors who try to bring healing to the wound of institutional estrangement from human experience. Countless people have been made to feel at odds with their own human nature and have, as a result, lived their lives in a sexually handicapped way, trying to follow institutional mandates and interpretations that by a perverse alchemy transform their naive human eroticism into something base and evil.

We mingle with these unnamed men and women every day, in the crowds that brush anonymously past us in big cities, labor above computers and drill presses, and may be seen through a thousand windows carrying out the ageless homely tasks of family life. Such people struggle to do their best under burdens made heavier by Church functionaries who, for what they construe to be good reasons, chronically misread and misinterpret their sexual natures and sexual experiences.

The unforgivable sin, the true sin against the Spirit, may well be to make people feel guilty about what is healthy in them— guilty, as charged, of being human. Those who commit this sin are always guilty of a companion fault as well. They mask what is sexually unhealthy in themselves, denying it while indulging and gratifying it in the actions they carry out complacently in the name of the Church.

THE SUFFERING SERVANT

Whenever the Church as an Institution—we will presently distinguish that from the Church as Mystery—attacks creativity in thought, imagination, or expression, it assaults the human energies that bring the achievement into being. Whenever this Church as an Institution suppresses human generativity, for example, in its authoritarian rejection of the renaissance of learning in scripture and theology at the beginning of the twentieth century or in the suppression of a ministry to gays at its very end, it never merely attacks an idea or a theory. It also assaults the thinker, the theorizer, or the minister—in short, the creator.

To this day, men and women who wish to remain in "good standing," as it is said, in the Institutional Church are forced to re-enact what we may term the Galileo Myth. They must surrender themselves—mind, heart, and will—to their accusers, disown their creation and often withdraw from creating, forsake their potency by giving up what they can bring forth from within themselves and, therefore, maim themselves intentionally and suicidally at the command of, and to gratify, the Institution. This sentence is better understood as an assault for no other word captures the violence with which it has been made on numerous theologians by the Congregation for the Doctrine of the Faith, once known as the Holy Office, under the leadership of Joseph Cardinal Ratzinger, who at the time of Vatican II was considered a highly creative theologian himself.

The sexual character of such transactions is laid bare in the verb used to describe what the Institution, through such departments, demands of such accused individuals. Men and women must *submit* and accept the conditions imposed on them that, in effect, desexualize them by numbing their creativity, forcing them to abort what they beget through their generativity. They must act against the life they give; reject and turn away from their own offspring, the fruit of their creativity; and live castrated lives.

Otherwise, such theologians and others will suffer ecclesiastical punishment that cannot easily be described other than as assailing the total personality of the creators. These are thorough punishments that would deny sheets to the dying and shrouds to the dead so that nothing might cover the intense shaming that the action intends to inflict. This profound humiliation is sexual in its intent and erotic in its gratification, as it aims not just to correct but to wound offenders in their generativity, in the sexually striated core energies of their being.

These outcomes include, as we shall see later in detail, symbolic castration that is real enough in its impact. Officials cut scholars off from the universe of their generativity by ousting them from academic faculties, forbidding them to write or speak on the subject of their expertise, and insisting on their accepting and keeping silent about changes in their creative work authored and imposed by others. Sometimes they are told, as the Swiss scholar Hans Kung and the American moralist Charles Curran were, that they can no longer call themselves *Catholic* theologians. That the sexuality at the core of this Galileo Myth is manipulative, unhealthy, and exploitative may be read in the debasement, humiliation, and shaming that characterize it.

We may be fully sympathetic to the long inventory of sexual suffering that is associated with the Institutional Church, but we cannot join ourselves to the official denying, looking away, temporizing, or in that truly last and worst of treasons, somehow adjusting to this monstrous distortion, learning nothing from it as, through these maneuvers, its credibility hemorrhages away so that it loses the strength even to call this by its rightful name.

In order to understand this unhealed, untreated, and unnamed wound, our lens must be that of the organizational culture that is its author and setting. We search the wound, as did the doctor to the Grail King; his "hand . . . found the spearhead therein, a splinter and the shaft as well, and removed them. . . . Whereupon [the king] was immediately borne through God's help to the Grail: but when he looked upon it his torture only increased, for he was now unable to die." But, as we learn in our passage together, this king—this Institution in pain—can be healed by the profound human and spiritual question of human concern that Parzival, matured by heterosexual love, asks in our foundational myth, "What is it that ails you?" This question symbolizes the pastoral resources of the Church as Mystery to address and heal the wound in the Church as Institution. Our reflections, therefore, do not forsake the official Church but allow us to invest ourselves and our hope in its recovery so that, healed itself, it will better heal the world.

PART TWO

. . . . .

BRICK AND MORTAR:
THE CHURCH AS
INSTITUTION

7

MYTHS OF INSTITUTIONAL
CATHOLICISM: BRICK AND MORTAR

✝

I N THE FIRST DECADES of the twentieth century, the Church in
the United States was vigorously involved in what has been
called its Brick and Mortar stage; aligning itself with the American Dream of its largely immigrant members, it built a new Eden
for them. The American Church seemed innocent as, supported by
its people, it supported them in turn, furnishing the Garden with
churches and schools and keeping the sheep away from the tree of
the knowledge of Good and Evil.

Much as it did more than a thousand years before, when the
Church defined itself by raising epic cathedrals across Europe, the
American Church entered the twentieth century closely identified
with what it built. If one could then view Chartres, Notre Dame, or
St. Peter's and read in the physical structure the glory and mystery
of Christianity, one could read its very American glory and success
in the structures anchored like triumphant fleets in the northern
industrial cities of the nation. American Catholicism celebrated
itself in brick and mortar everywhere. A pastor served as priest and
clerk of the works as these churches and schools rose around him.
The Chicago Catholic school system became the fourth largest of
all school systems, secular or religious, in the United States.

This vast, gloried deployment of buildings both reinforced and
expressed the theme of the Church as an institution, a "physical
plant" in which, as in the archdiocese of New York, the metaphor
was unconsciously extended by routine references to the Chancery

Office as "the Power House." This supported and also reflected the hierarchical grading of the universe in which the heavens were split off from the earth. So, too, the highest, and the holiest, were on the upper strata of the steppe-like society of the Church. The Institution's working definition of human personality arose from its almost unquestioned model of the divided self, the spirit fettered by the flesh. This assumption of a basic cleft in the cosmos was also expressed in everyday devotions and religious language. The Institution fashioned literal points of reference as physical and fixed as the holy water font. Heaven was *above*, prayer was offered *up*, Hell was *below*, and two great teachings—the *Ascension* of Jesus and the *Assumption* of Mary—were presented in literal, rather than spiritual, formulations, according to this map of reality. Virtue breathed in the pure air of the highest peaks (recall the *mount* of Perfection), while vice inhaled the sulphurous fumes of the *pit* of Hell.

The Institutional Church also conceptualized itself in the imagery of a dying age as a literal "kingdom." The feast of Christ the King, of Jesus in royal robes regnant over the earth, was established only in the nineteenth century, an unambiguous signal of how the institution remained insulated, or divided off, from the world in which the foundations of hierarchy and its empires were already being undermined by history. This dividing line drawn across creation was thought as natural and even as noble as the saber scars in the militaristic Prussia of the same era. The last autocrats, Kaiser Wilhelm, with his withered arm, and Tsar Nicholas, with hemophilia in the blood, were kings as maimed and destined for death as their mythic forebears. They grimly heralded the end of the hierarchical authority they sought to preserve, that divine right of kings on whose high altar they made a bloody sacrifice of millions of lives.

The hierarchical imagination took as divine illumination the vaporous Northern Lights that were the last traces of a vanishing religious and physical cosmos, leaving wounds bricked over by the ecclesiastical structure in its frenzied era of building. Sealed within was the truth about the complex unity of personality, including sex and gender, the oneness of our beings as saints or sinners. This misconceived Eden was, above all, in the confident masculine opinion of the clerical culture that dominated the Church, a man's world.

THE AMERICAN DREAM

The bishops entered the American myth themselves, boasting of what they took pride in, the "parish plants," as they were termed, that were counterparts in their towers and in the national energy they expressed of the automotive and other factories also spreading, like the Church itself, around big northern cities. In fact, the bishops, as organizational executives, ate freely and unwittingly the forbidden fruit, losing their managerial innocence as they became twins to capitalists, as confident as America's bankers and moguls in the future of the country.

This period represented the zenith of the American Church as a hierarchy and its cardinals as great prince bishops. The Catholic people, a generation and more away from affluence, purchased self-esteem with the pennies they gave willingly to allow their leaders to live as well as their opposite numbers—the Morgans, the Rockefellers, and the Schwabs—in the capitalist class. It is hard to imagine now, but at that time such conspicuous consumption added a frisson of romance to the lives and habits of bishops, who often understood themselves as American success stories—the successors, as they thought and think still of themselves, of the apostles, spiritual inheritors with a taste for acquiring worldly goods.

If, for example, William Cardinal O'Connell had returned from Rome in 1901 to an assignment in Portland, Maine, which preceded his later becoming archbishop of Boston, with an entourage that included a coachman, a valet, and a music master, he came to personify the bishop as a classic American success story. He obscured his own tenement boyhood, reinventing it as a bucolic delight in a book whose copies he had shoveled into the furnace of the archiepiscopal residence after a local newspaperman discovered its rewrite of history. Not only had he built a large, antique-filled residence in Boston, but he further signaled his identification with the Brahmin class by maintaining a winter home in the Bahamas and a summer one at Marblehead. So often did he travel to the former that his priests referred to him as "Gangplank Bill." On the edge of the Cape, he strode the beach in his flat black hat and frock coat, his episcopal chain glinting in the sun, his gleaming limousine trolling the sands behind him. This is straight-out American mythology, part Horatio Alger and part Before the Fall.

George Cardinal Mundelein was a Brooklyn boy who became archbishop of Chicago where he lived in the regal style of such European-struck Americans as publisher William Randolph Hearst. He transported treasures from the Continent and re-created Roman sites and scenes, such as the Barberini bees he set swarming on the library ceiling of his country estate seminary forty miles north of his many-chimneyed mansion on the city's North Side. On the seminary grounds, he slept in a brick-trimmed replica of Mount Vernon and was driven back and forth to Chicago in a limousine with crimson-strutted wheels. Along the curving seminary's drive his coat of arms bloomed in a huge shield of flowers. His seminarians lived in another world as well. Mostly sons of immigrants, they were thought to have a "higher" calling than their siblings and were housed in Georgian brick buildings and spent their summers in a villa four hundred miles north on the shores of Lake Michigan. It cannot be denied that this Church had a sense of place.

The everyday clerical conversation among bishops and priests in heavily Catholic cities, such as Chicago, Detroit, and Boston, expressed the physical analogues of ecclesiastical achievement. Territory bestowed identity, and ordinary Catholics located one another not by asking the name of their town but of their parish. This was raised to a magisterial level by bishops who referred to themselves and one another not by their own names but by those of their dioceses. In the early 1950s Samuel Cardinal Stritch of Chicago, for example, could tell an aide in his Hobe Sound, Florida, retreat that "Chicago will visit Detroit today," meaning that he intended to visit Edward Cardinal Mooney of the Motor City at his nearby winter residence. Bishop Bryan McEntagart, transferred in 1957 from being rector of the Catholic University of America in Washington, D.C., to head the diocese of Brooklyn, employed a well-known clerical phrase when he told a fellow bishop, "It's good to have my feet under my own table again." The symbol of a man's leaving the priesthood, a rare and socially punishing event at that time, was nonetheless told in material terms as his "turning in his cup and book."

The ecclesiastical shorthand of the day reflected how identity and accomplishment were equated with a physical object, from the breviary, the obligatory daily prayer of priests that was called "the wife" to the "red hat" of cardinals to the "tub of butter" into which pastors of wealthy parishes gladly settled themselves. The cardinals were "hinges" (from *cardo*, "hinge") to the great door of a vast structure. The Church's annual reports used material transfers and numbers as efficiently as a shipping company to describe dioceses' spiritual condition. The sacramental life of the Church was reported under such titles as "Number of Communions Received," "Number of Masses Said."

In the everyday devotional life of the Church, this mathematical reduction of spirituality was incorporated into what were termed "Spiritual Bouquets." These, whose modern counterpart may be found in underwriting "Walks" for various causes, presented gifts for the spiritual benefit of another, listing pledges of such activities as "Number of Rosaries Recited," "Number of Visits to the Blessed Sacrament," and "Number of Masses Heard." This quasi-monetized spirituality was a function of this divided model of creation that necessitated a translation of religion into the counterpart of brick and mortar. Calculations as complicated as tax deductions went into the reckoning of the number of "years" or "days" in Purgatory (three hundred days for this, a year for that) remitted through reciting some prayer or performing some devotion. These were the residual form of Indulgences whose outright sale in the sixteenth century first led Martin Luther to search his conscience about the Institutional Church. Nobody seemed to notice that this formulaic rendering of the spiritual into the material, possible only because of a deep split in the ecclesiastical view of the world, led to the still-unhealed wound of the Church that we call the Reformation.

DEATH OF THE SALESMEN

Pastors enjoyed unalloyed authoritarian power during this Brick and Mortar phase of American Catholic life. Once they got what they called "a place of my own," they had life tenure and often felt fulfilled only if they built something—a new church, a gym, a meeting hall—that gave outward expression to their sense of inner grace. In large dioceses priests might serve as assistants for thirty years and were often wounded knights in one way or another by the time they achieved the Grail of becoming pastors. These priests often paid the price to support this idealized hierarchical structure by functioning obediently at its lowest level but one, the bottom occupied by ordinary Catholics, whose calling was less noble than theirs.

Big Business had, in fact, adopted the strictly hierarchical "command and control" model of the military after the Civil War. Both the business and the military abandoned this approach long before the millennium loomed. CEOs across America have been experimenting expensively for the last generation with new management structures, ranging from offices without walls to organizations without central headquarters, to replace hierarchy. Some have adopted the collegial model that Vatican II brought back to the Church a generation before Big Business realized that hierarchy no longer worked.

Here the bishops' unlikely brotherhood with the CEOs ends, as do their roles in the great American Dream whose reflected allure they once shared. Now the bishops are estranged from the business-leader class, who have chosen to experiment with instability at the center while the Pope attempts the opposite by resurrecting hierarchy. America has fallen in love with entrepreneurs whose Information Age invention has doomed hierarchy. So America's bishops, called upon by Rome to be faithful supporters of hierarchy, live—more uncomfortably every day—in a world that regards hierarchy as it does the Eiffel Tower, a curio that whispers of a long-gone time.

They are left, one might note, with the leftovers of the Brick and Mortar Age in which so much about the Church, in its private workings and its public presence, was identified with the physical. Seminaries and religious houses that were expanded many times over in the immediate post–World War II period stand empty, for sale, or converted to other uses across the land. The estates that various religious groups purchased for their training houses are now occupied by unexpected successor owners. Followers of Sung Ying Moon now fill the corridors where black-robed aspirants once processed gravely at Tarrytown, New York.

Not far above in the Hudson Valley, close by the silent graveyard where Pierre Teilhard de Chardin lies buried among a regiment of forgotten confreres, the Culinary Institute of America now operates in the cluster of buildings once known as St. Andrew's, one of the most esteemed Jesuit training houses in the United States. Large churches, as big as the cathedrals back in the European cities from which immigrant Catholics once flooded into America, now stand empty, too expensive to heat, the Catholic school amalgamated with one nearby, great symbols of great come-and-get-it days for Catholics being closed down in every big city.

These structures give quiet and melancholy testimony to that era in which the Church was closely and successfully identified with its institutional personality.

MYTHS OF THE PRIESTHOOD

The myths of the priesthood of that era may be found, of course, in the work of writers, playwrights, and filmmakers. The chronic vassal's state of priests whose youthful enthusiasm faded, knights wounded during decades of waiting to become pastors, was chronicled in the brilliant short stories and novels of J. F. Powers. He won the National Book Award for fiction for *Morte d'Urban*, a near perfect evocation of the career of a priest fund-raiser, a success and a tragedy for a figure who could be a cousin to Willy Loman.

In these tales one finds the unvarnished clerical culture of midcentury America and what men's lives are like when they are totally dominated by an institution that seems to be at the height of its accomplishment when, in fact, it has already begun its descent to a period in which history, like Samson, shook the pillars and, amid these closed parishes, schools, and seminaries, brought an end to the Brick and Mortar mythology. These vivid characters are men adjusting variously to domination by a total institution that, along with other American hierarchies, was in the Eisenhower era on the verge of structural decline and spiritual renewal.

There was, in the heyday of the building period, an entirely different oeuvre of myth about American priests, one far more in accord with the dream of free-market achievement. A sharp division was apparent between the public and private roles of the priest. The latter was taken to be pure, as the priest had a "higher" vocation than his brother, the policeman or the alderman. It was protected, and its real dynamics—especially those concerning priests' conflicts over their own sex and gender identity—were never raised and were explored only by those professionals who were expected to manage priestly falls from grace with the utmost discretion. If priests were judged good or lived long enough, they could be made monsignors, counterparts to lower-court figures in the age of royalty. Romanticized priests were thought to be Knights of the Grail, noble and pure in every way. Papal honors made men and women into Knights and Ladies of Malta or of the Holy Sepulchre. A magazine for altar boys was called *Knights of the Altar*. The myth of the Grail and the American Dream overlapped.

TRUE CONFESSIONS

This romanticization of the hierarchically exalted bishop as a destined all-American inheritor, along with hierarchically installed company chairman, to the American Dream was reflected in Henry Morton Robinson's novel, *The Cardinal*, published halfway through the twentieth century and said to have been inspired by O'Connell. The physical object of the red hat had become the Grail equivalent in this emergent myth of American Catholicism. Becoming mythical, however, involves one in unforeseen trials and inescapable destinies, as we will presently see.

This idyllic Church in which every mother might dream that her finest son could become a cardinal was revised by another American novelist, John Gregory Dunne, in his 1977 masterpiece, *True Confessions*. Here are characters who match those of Robinson's work but possess a specific gravity that the latter's idealized clerics lack. They are as recognizable as those of J. F. Powers, but the myth, refined in the fire of Dunne's imagination, has taken on a color as true as that of the confessions of the title.

Dunne shifts the locale, as the power of the Church had spread, westward to the untended Eden of Los Angeles, where the handsome and talented priest Monsignor Desmond Spellacy completes the mythological journey to its tragic but redemptive stage. He and his once bright chances of promotion are symbolically slain by his Homicide Squad brother, Tom, who uncovers the reeking corruption, the hypocrisy, and murder of the Brick and Mortar Catholicism, that deceptive Eden from which Monsignor Spellacy is exiled to the biblical desert of Twenty-Nine Palms.

Fittingly, the corruption erupts from the Brick and Mortar Church in which bishops and Big Businessmen shook hands on their roles in the American Dream and ate its proffered apple and could never be innocent again. *The Cardinal* tracks the sunny side of the dream, while *True Confessions* tracks its shadow as it spreads over the second-generation Irish Catholics who earn their exile from the Garden by their unoriginal sins of lust, greed, and murder. There is no hint of the fairy-tale scene in *The Cardinal* in which it is observed that the new Prince of the Church would have no ring had his parents not pledged their love with another kind of ring first.

Dunne's *True Confessions* is a mythological rendering of loss and redemption, of salvation for sinners who might be cast out of the Church as an Institution but could always have a place in the Church as a People. In this myth we recognize the story of the American priesthood as it reflects the story, largely of the flawed paradise of Brick and Mortar Catholicism that has, for the best institutional reasons, resisted insight into the heart of its central conflicted dynamics. It has preferred to deny or to suppress, for example, the ambivalent and often immature sexuality, the unhealed wound beneath so much of its uneasy clerical ambition and maneuver, even though it may be observed in the agony of a thousand Desmond Spellacys.

8

ROMANTICIZED DISCIPLINE:
WOMEN DO THE SUFFERING

☩

T HE ERA OF BUILDING may have been ideal for sublimating the sexuality of many bishops and priests whose potency was challenged and, to some extent, expressed by the game, almost as exclusive as Friday-night poker, of raising funds and towers for the Church as an institution. Building was not a subtle process, but with hands alternately smoothed and toughened by the touch of blueprints and bricks, a man might feel that he had earned a drink before dinner. This heavy masculine character of the age was filled with rewards for men. Not the least of these, however, arose from the male domination of women, a given of that period in the culture in general and in the Church in particular.

This presumption of singular male potency was written into canon law, which forbade a woman's ever being the superior, in theory, of a large religious order that she might, in fact, be running with great skill. Only a male figure could hold the superior's position, even if he had nothing to do with its function, because women were not thought, by the law that reflected institutional psychology, canonically capable of exercising authority within what was imagined and described as the "perfect society" of the Church. The requirements for ordination for the priesthood made the case in stark fashion: *mas baptizatus* (a baptized male). There was no other specification about qualifications or education. A baptized male would do.

This, and other habits of the clerical mind beyond counting, maintained women in a subordinate position, as if they were not a gender unto themselves but the "spoiled male"—female by defect in conception—that even Saint Thomas, following Aristotle, considered them to be. Men alone were capable of exercising *potestas*, as it was called, power in the Church. On a vulgar level, Catholic men borrowed a line from the locker-room culture that asserted the same theme of masculine potency and innate superiority when they laughingly clinked their glasses and spoke of keeping their wives "barefoot and pregnant."

This was memorably reflected by such men of goodwill as Jesuit Gerald Kelly, the moral theologian whose *Modern Youth and Chastity*, published in 1941, set the ideals, the tone, and the norms for anything and everything sexual in American Catholic life. Kelly was a well-trained and highly intelligent man who lived, although unobservant of his woundedness, in the Brick and Mortar culture, as isolated as the Grail King in his castle but unaware of his plight or that his need for healing was as great as that of the Catholics wounded by him.

Here is a good man so possessed by the Catholic culture that he cannot notice the profound condescension toward women with which his opinions are imbued. His attitude was Everyman's attitude in that period, so he reflects broader cultural assumptions filtered through Catholic teaching. In writing of marriage, he treats gender expectations and characteristics by asserting that men are attracted by grace, emotional susceptibility, beauty, and tenderness. Women are drawn by courage, strength, energy, and calm deliberation. The questions a man should ask when seeking a wife include "Can she cook, and make a house a home?" "Has she that womanly quality that instinctively puts things in order?" He recapitulates approvingly a story from the *Notre Dame Bulletin* about a man who leaves a broom on the floor of his room. After five women stepped over it, one finally picked it up. "The wise man," he concludes, "proposed [to the sixth]—and there is much to be said for this wisdom."[1]

A MAN'S WORLD: SEXUAL MORALITY

If this is emblematic of the division between the Church as a controlling institution and its women as subordinate actors to be controlled, one must also note how even moral reflections on sexuality, including marital sexuality, were reserved for a celibate clergy who felt that such exclusivity was justified by their role as the judges of sins. Hoarding information at the top of the pyramid is classic hierarchical behavior. Such "eyes only" handling of information was an exercise less of discretion than of unrefined and unbleached power.

Information in hierarchies is considered a stock good rather than a flow good and is placed on the highest shelf of hierarchy, to which only the powerful few have access. Indeed, such information was equated with power as it was kept away from and used against those on lower rungs of the organizational ladder. The essential character of information as a flow good has become evident in the Space Information Age that has obliterated the middle and left what were once high and low on the same plane.

Still, this "Holy of Holies" approach that reserved access to sexual information and decision making to only male clerics provides us with an operational definition of the unhealed wound, that ozone layer–like hole at the top of a hierarchy that cannot be permitted to heal and become healthy. Healing is a threat, as sunshine and fresh air are to the damp and cobwebbed dark, because health not only shakes off the unwarranted control of others but also frustrates the latter's vicarious gratifications.

Thus, in the textbooks of Moral Theology that began to appear in English in that period, discussion of sexual matters reflected the wound by its sharp separation from the rest of the text in a discrete section and in Latin, then the language of the clergy. The power to judge and resolve the cases, all of which concerned laypeople, belonged to male clerics alone. This division was reinforced by the explicit policies of such journals as the *American Ecclesiastical Review,* in which sexual cases were analyzed in a clinical manner for use by priests in the confessional, perhaps not so accidentally a darkened venue in which the confessor exercised what was termed the "power" to forgive sins. As Leslie Griffin notes, "The editors . . . explain that they try to limit subscriptions to priests and students of theology. . . . There is also concern that certain suggestive materials should not be accessible to lay readers."[2]

The case system, in which the principals were so often designated *Caius* and *Bertha* and their sexual sins were revealed as so various that they became subjects of M*A*S*H-like clerical badinage, depended on the opinions of writers of manuals, not on basic theological research. Such "casuistry . . . relies on theological opinions for questions which are open to dispute. . . . Attention is paid to *acts* and to the *sinfulness of certain acts* [emphasis added]."[3]

This emphasis on acts was challenged by the Dominican scholars Charles Callan and John McHugh in their 1929 work, *Moral Theology* (2 vols., New York: Jos. Wagner), in which they emphasize principles rather than opinions. This humane work speaks of the "life of grace and virtue" as an escape from the previous underscoring of "moral disease and death." Even here, however, the fundamental wound is apparent in the assertion that "sex pleasure has been ordained by God as an inducement to perform an act which is both disgusting in itself and burdensome in its consequences."[4]

Truly burdensome were the distinctions that flowed from the divided model of the human being, so obvious in the quotation above from Callan and McHugh, theologians considered moderate and understanding during the long boom era of Brick and Mortar Catholicism and brought to a fine point in the tables of Gerald Kelly. In his *Modern Youth and Chastity*, which was profoundly influential in the 1940s and 1950s, he analyzes violations of the Commandments:

For the Sixth Commandment:

MORTAL SIN   **a.** All directly venereal actions.

                       b. All other actions performed for the

purpose of stimulating or promoting venereal pleasure.

c. All actions involving the proximate
danger of performing a directly venereal
action or of consenting to venereal pleasure.

VENIAL SIN   **a.** Indirectly venereal actions performed
without a relatively sufficient reason.

NO SIN   **a.** Indirectly venereal actions performed
with a relatively sufficient reason.

For the Ninth Commandment:

MORTAL SIN   **a.** The *wilful approval* of unchaste actions.
b. The wilful entertaining of any thoughts
for the purpose of stimulating or promoting
venereal passion.
c. The wilful harboring of thoughts which
involve the *proximate danger* of performing
an unchaste action, or consenting to venereal pleasure.

VENIAL SIN   **a.** Thinking about sexually stimulating
things without a sufficient reason.

NO SIN   **a.** Thinking about sexually stimulating
things with a sufficient reason.[5]

Kelly wants nothing more than to be helpful to people. Yet the tension of this approach—presuming a lighthouse structure of personality, in which the beacon of the intellect at its top obsessively
sweeps across the inferior structure and the dark impinging sea—
rises still from one of his examples of a Ninth Commandment mortal sin:

Mary once committed the sin of fornication, and now she thinks about that action, and wilfully rejoices over the fact that she committed it. In other words, Mary, instead of having sorrow for the sin as she should have, here and now goes over it again in her mind with wilful approval of what she did.

SINFUL MARY, SINLESS MARY

Mary here stands for Everywoman, for it was woman, clerics confidently averred, through whom sin came into the world: Eve, temptress in Eden; Eve, temptress now. The ambivalence with which women were perceived during the great Brick and Mortar period merely echoed a long tradition of male discomfort with, and fear of, women. Exceptions were Mary, the mother of Jesus, and the mothers of bishops and priests.

The desexualization of Mary, by which she was purified of every erotic desire or longing, much less sin, also allowed her to become a mother without experiencing passionate love or a sexual relationship and to give birth while still a virgin, uncontaminated by the condition or consequences of being human. One may retain great devotion to Mary, the mother of Jesus, without forcing her into asexuality, the antiseptic condition in which she was celebrated. Any effort to explore Mary as a sexual being, or even to open the possibility that this eradication of generative sexuality in her life may have wounded her reality and the sexual sensibility of the untold generations who have called her blessed, would be rejected angrily by institutional officials who would judge this to be sacrilegious and heretical.

A title sometimes ascribed to Mary is Queen of the Clergy, and while this seems benevolent, it may also shield a sexual dynamic that has been as pervasive and powerful as it has been unexamined among the Catholic priests who held the keys to bind or loosen sexual sins. It is of no small significance that, in the clerical culture, the priest's mother achieved an extraordinary position, attested to by the saying, commonplace among them, that "you never lose the son who becomes a priest." To another woman, that is.

To this day, this relationship remains a principal one in many regions of the contemporary Catholic culture. This preservation of an original psychological bond with the mother figure, unmodified by any later, different, and deeper relationship with a woman, has profoundly shaped the clerical psyche and the clerical imagination of the world. Working through a more adult relationship with the opposite sex is, however, essential if the man, a priest in our consideration, is to separate successfully from his earliest relationships and achieve heterosexual individuation and independence.

For generations, however, priests were told that celibacy meant that they could have no close relationships with women, that these were inevitably "occasions of sin." This advice may have been well meant, and it was almost impossible to question because it would bring a man into conflict with the massed power of the Institutional Church on which he was totally dependent for his identity, his license to function, as it were, and his daily sustenance. Beneath this discipline we may observe the invisible but real transaction between institution and subject: the organization thereby wounded the priest in his manhood as surely as Anfortas and Tristan had been, emasculating him as Abelard had been.

Nonetheless, many healthy priests do develop healthy relationships with women and other persons in their work and thereby grow out of their good-boy role. Others, however, never grow past this and have only fleeting glimpses of the sexual and gender confusions and conflicts that are their unhealed wounds and the source of much anguish and sorrow for them. Mother, however, was always safe, well into her old age as long as the priest could remain psychologically a boy into his middle age.

It is not surprising to discover in clerics, and their attitudes toward sex, the unobserved effects of incomplete relationships with women. It is also significant to observe that in the great age of building, the relationship of priest and mother was both heavily sentimentalized and widely approved. It was even celebrated, as it was in 1944's Academy Award–winning film, *Going My Way*, in which it served as the emotional climax of the story. Walking away into the snowy night—a perfect if unconsciously wrought celibate symbolization of a man, self-sufficient and alone, heading into the cold, uncomforted dark—Father O'Malley has left one gift for the old pastor, Father Fitzgibbons, whose church finances he has also put to right. He has brought the pastor's ancient mother back from Ireland, silver-haired, gloved, and dressed in black, for a warm embrace and reunion with her aging son. It is dramatically effective and was applauded at the time, even though, reviewed half a century and more later, it is a powerful evocation of the one profound emotional relationship permitted to priests that was, sadly for all, wounding as well.

CARDINAL VIRTUES

In Robinson's *The Cardinal* we find a clear example of how men, secure in their relationships with their mothers and confident of their judgmental roles in the Church, could make decisions about women's lives without even consulting them. This is the split made wide as a canal in personality, gender relationships, and regard—and within the Church itself as an Institution. Here we also see the lines, like the tracery on a palimpsest, of a struggle yet to come, of men's ecclesiastical control of their sexuality against which women would rebel, much to the astonishment of the clergy, later in the century.

Robinson's novel offers a view of the romanticized discipline of that era when it was taken for granted that men would make the gravest decisions affecting women in every area, including whether they would live or die in childbirth. The cardinal's surgeon brother-in-law will not perform a craniotomy during the birth of a child with "too large a head." Too late for other procedures, such as a cesarean section, both mother and child die. The cardinal, presented here in heroic mold, supports the decision, even though it is the surgeon who pays the price for it by being sued by the dead woman's surviving husband and losing his credentials at the hospital after refusing to sign an agreement that in the future he will follow indicated medical procedures.

In the midst of this, the cleric hero prays, "If this trial comes to me, Lord, grant that I may not murmur against the great severity of your love." With dramatic inevitability, Mona, his favorite sibling, later goes into labor, and a different surgeon tells the prelate, "If you don't give me permission to kill the embryo, there is nothing that can save your sister." The cardinal hero "clutches his chair: 'Jesus, Mary, and Joseph, stand by me.'" Then, without talking to his sister, he decides to let her die and to let the baby live.

This represents the romanticization of the suffering allotted to women by the sexual morality of that era in which the clerical figure who heads the institution is presented as having done the right thing, the hard thing, identified in his interior monologue; his prayer is not *whether* he should let his sister die but that he may have the strength to do so and thus carry out his moral duty. This was considered heroic, man's work, indeed, in the heyday of the Brick and Mortar Church. It was a moral decision as clear as a blueprint, and so wide was the gulf of worthiness that stretched between male and female that to question or examine it could not enter the consciousness of the cardinal or of the culture in which he was approved as a manly leader. The moral test is understood as not for her but for him, this knight of another time who, seeking the Grail of higher Church honors, unaware that he is re-enacting the battle between the Guardian of the Spirit and the Heathen Knight of Nature, slays the latter—for is not his moral code a triumph of Supernature over Nature?—and does not understand that he has been wounded or why it will not heal.

ASEXUALITY IN ACTION:
THE CURIAL STYLE

✝

ONE OF THE MOST important courses taken by young clerics destined for Roman degrees and careers, first as secretaries, or minutante, and perhaps later as monsignors and archbishops, in the administrative Church is one in the *stylus curiae*, the style of the Curia, that collective noun for all the congregations that carry out the Vatican's daily business (for example, the Doctrine of the Faith, better known and not so long ago as the Holy Office, the headquarters of the Roman Inquisition). This course in language and customs acclimates the beginning cleric as it indoctrinates him with the manners and mode in which the Institutional Church thinks and speaks to and about itself.

A language at once formal and restrained, this native tongue of the Church as an Institution controls the manner of reflection and communication that neutralizes the passion attached to many issues, such as the famous "rites" question that arose when, five hundred years ago, the first Catholic missionaries to China pleaded to have the liturgy accommodated to the language and customs of a then receptive Far East. The request was denied, a great opportunity of evangelization was forever lost to the Church, and history itself, we may say, was profoundly affected.

This issue, to which deep feelings remained attached, boiled over again a hundred years ago, to be settled finally by a delegate representing the Vatican—American Dennis Dougherty—in the 1930s, effectively closing off the possibilities of such adaptation to another culture. It took an ecumenical council, Vatican II, to renew the liturgy and allow its celebration in the vernacular and to permit other indigenous religious symbolism and practices to be incorporated into worship in the local churches throughout the world. The style of the Curia could be observed not only in the autocratic, plenipotentiary power with which Dougherty was invested but in the barricaded finality of the settlement, *Roma locuta est, causa finita est.* All participants were sworn, under the threat of penalties temporal and eternal, to secrecy. No appeal or further discussion of the matter was possible. In short, the curial style in operation. Dougherty was later named the cardinal archbishop of Philadelphia.

Classically, this curial approach, like that of other world-hardened entities, accepts its losses, even if they are half the world, for the Orient was half the world away from the Curia's foundations rising from the eternal stones of Rome. This mode of resolving such issues and dealing with people serves the interests of the administrative Church, whether in the short run the decision is fair or unfair or, indeed, in the long run good or bad for the Church as religious Mystery. Much as trading in stocks makes money for the broker whether people are buying or selling, or whether the value is gaining or losing, this style reinforces itself every time it is employed.

While good men of benevolent intention function in this interconnected bureaucracy, they are convinced that such losses must be accepted to ensure gains for the administrative control of the Church. Such losses, even of kingdoms, are the fruit of a temporal order that is separate from and antagonistic to the Church. This mirrors the division, inlaid as finely as Vatican marble in the administrative imagination, of body and soul, spirit and flesh as eternal opponents. The *stylus curiae* expresses, in its low-key obsessiveness, a Church completely confident that it has an eternal mandate, that God, as both Allies and Germans claimed in World War I, is on its side.

The uncomfortable acquiescence demanded of its greater and

lesser officials in decisions that conflict with their consciences wrenches something from their souls. They must look away from the human suffering that results from declaring, for example, that homosexuals carry within themselves "an objective disorder." On the basis of odds and averages, this assessment applies to more than a few of the officials who sign off on such judgments. Furthermore, this moral diagnosis is based, if such foundation exists at all, on a weak theological, scriptural, and psychological basis. How can these men say their prayers and go to the office every day?

They pay a price, hidden from themselves, beneath a master motive for all those who may be termed Churchmen, that is, men of the Church. They are comforted by the powerful rationalization that God is always writing straight with their crooked lines. They do everything, swallowing the bitter with the sweet, "for the good of the Church." This ennobling and unanswerable sentiment may well be the principal mantra of the careerist element, no small segment, of the institution. The curial style depends on and yet is also undone by its ability to depersonalize the most intensely personal issues, including human love and sexuality.

It is in this style that we recognize some of the sexual dynamics that, like a rocket arching from the *Titanic* over a silent sea, tell us that a human drama filled with every possibility of heartbreak is being enacted, that men and women fill the night with their cries just beyond the horizon and beyond our hearing.

THE PILATE SYNDROME

This signature motif of the myth of the institutional or clerical priesthood—and, indeed, of all those classes of men and women characterized as "subjects" in the "perfect society" staked out by canon law—is that of power, often masked as authority, exercised almost intuitively for purposes of control. The true nature of this style—the energies of the human transactions that it governs—has seldom been examined, even though it has been used ruthlessly and regularly throughout history.

In the Church as Institution, administrators have done grave and damaging things to the men who are priests while evincing an official innocence and self-absolution very like Pilate's washing his hands and cleansing himself of responsibility for the fate of Jesus. In fact, they often are innocent by reasons of sanity, that is, by their rational obedience to practices whose irrationality they have been conditioned never to question. Such ecclesiastical leaders truly believe that they are carrying out a divinely imposed duty in a divinely ordained way in a hierarchically deployed Church, in which they view the playing field from the equivalent of sky boxes. They mean well; they are, by their lights, doing the "right" thing because they are carrying out their providential obligation to ensure and promote what they understand, in a famous phrase, as "the good of the Church."

That notion, dependent on a divided view of the world, remains operative to this very day and is, psychologically speaking, very powerful in its effects on the bishops and other mid-hierarchy managers who are convinced that they are exercising *legitimate authority* when they are actually applying *power legitimated* by their unconscious rationalization of it as God's good will for the Church. This was expressed, in the Brick and Mortar heyday, in the dramatic oratory of Bishop Fulton J. Sheen in the principle "Right is right when nobody else is right, and wrong is wrong when everybody else is wrong."

It is understandable that such leaders would feel an afterglow from performing loyally, their burden made light by their expectation that their dutifulness is appreciated by someone at a higher level. There is nothing distinctively ecclesiastical about this Pilate Syndrome. It may be observed wherever the game of politics is played, from municipalities to universities and perhaps, as an old Irish saying put it, in hell itself.

That such power is to authority as lust is to love suggests what those who expend it may never suspect, that unacknowledged sexual need explains the complex gratification that flows from men exercising power over other men. The outer purpose always sounds noble, to defend the Church's teaching authority—or the Magisterium, as it is called—and to nip the first buds of dissent lest they bloom as heresy. Indeed, the reason for and the outcome of employing power is often described in the vocabulary of chastity: doctrine must remain "pure," Holy Mother Church, as it is called, cannot be "defiled" by false teaching or errant behavior, papal teaching authority cannot be "violated."

Whatever it may be called, the underlying psychological and spiritual reality is not difficult to recognize. Men use power against other men in order to destroy their masculine potency. This ecclesiastical eugenics is designed to eliminate their capacity to reproduce themselves in their ideas. Feeling righteous is a totalitarian emotion and justifies wounding men in their manhood, emasculating them in the name of an institution that does not notice the shadow it casts as it focuses on and overwhelms them. Women must also be controlled and kept in their place, but men—the potent male—must be incapacitated, ruined as a man, and shamed and humiliated as well. Howsoever it has been described or in whatever supposedly spiritual disguise it appears, this movement of men to overcome other men has been profoundly sexual in its root energies. Observe the involuntary tic, the sudden tenseness, and the flares in every Pilate's eyes when the lash first draws blood from the bare back of the prisoner. What lies beneath this Pilate Syndrome if not a manifest need for symbolic purification to forestall looking more deeply into actions that substitute for, or vicariously express, the clouded, undeveloped, or suppressed sexuality of those who carry them out?

THE SILENCE OF THE SHEPHERDS

Healthy bishops sense the brutality in such transactions, which they are pushed to perform to prove that they are true to their being chosen, as they understand it, from all eternity by the Spirit, and at some level they must swallow their own shame to demonstrate their own orthodoxy. The health in such men bids them to pull back from what, if assented to wholeheartedly, means their emasculation. Many healthy superiors and bishops are, in fact, violated within by the orders they are expected to carry out.

Other Church officials, less healthy by half, especially those who "make a career" in its bureaucracy, respond readily because such actions sustain, as fouled creeks do a polluted river, their own sexually toned personality needs, that is, needs that might horrify them if they identified these as their own drive to control or to dominate others. Far from being "light in the darkness," as some of them esteem their intentions, this profound and, to them, mostly hidden dynamic is a wire fallen inside them whose dangerous energy charges much of the so-called restoration now being carried out with the help of the kind of willing, if often unknowing, accomplices that authoritarianism always enlists.

That Brick and Mortar Church was confident of its newly codified canonical authority (1917) and expressed this sureness—take it or leave it—in the laws of which the priest was the agent and the enforcer. Many priests were themselves humiliated by the humiliations they ordered on their flocks: the estrangement of families from a divorced member, an institutionally supported shunning of them, the refusal of Catholic burial to publicly designated sinners, the indignities imposed in "mixed" marriages that were discussed by theologians as "occasions of sin" (in which the non-Catholic spouse might tempt the Catholic to use birth control, and so be weakened in faith) and therefore could not be celebrated inside the altar rail and sometimes not even in the Church.

How many Catholic families might identify with the alienating and embittering experience that the famous actor James Cagney described about his father's last illness in turn-of-the-century Manhattan? His father's heavy drinking contributed to his early death, but when Cagney was sent by his mother to get the priest for the last sacraments, the priest told him that he would not come unless he was paid first. The Cagney family left the Church, and the actor remained estranged until John Cardinal O'Connor of New York made an effort to reconcile him before his death in 1986. Indeed, in O'Connor's plea at the actor's funeral mass, for forgiveness for the Church for having so injured his family so many years before, one could hear a rare admission of how destructive the miscarriage of clerical power could be.

When the institution was tightly bound in brick and mortar, one could also read, in the troubled souls of priests called to justify heartbreak in the name of faith, as well as in the moral complacency of their bishops or confreres, the lockstep religious drama of the era, prisoner shackled to guard in an endless last mile. One of its symbols appeared in Catholic papers as the "Question Box" column in which a priest responded to queries about Catholic life: subjects that were obviously of radically differing moral character—eating meat on Fridays, using birth control, doing "servile work" on Sundays, failing to banish sexual thoughts, committing murder—were treated as mortal sins, each equal to the other in gravity, that, unforgiven and unrepented of, opened hell's furnace to the offenders. In popular American Catholic culture, the "Question Box" was the equivalent of *Roma locuta est, causa finita est*, Rome has spoken, the matter is settled.

ANNALS OF EMASCULATION

Brick and Mortar Catholicism was an all-encompassing structure that kept guards at each entrance and exit and willingly acceded to Roman congregations, carrying out their rules with at least as much confidence in their letter as in the spirit that supposedly animated them. Just before his death, the priest-scholar acknowledged to be the dean of Catholic historians, Monsignor John Tracy Ellis, suggested that twentieth-century American Catholicism could best be understood in a classic essay by Dr. Michael V. Gannon that was part of the historical review of the American priesthood underwritten by the National Conference of Catholic Bishops immediately after Vatican II concluded. "It's all in there," Ellis said of Professor Gannon's study, *Before and After Modernism: The Intellectual Isolation of the American Priest.*[1]

This account of an extraordinary period in American Catholic history—whose existence is, except to scholars, virtually unknown—tells of the surge of intellectual interest and activity at the end of the nineteenth century that, had it not been brutally suppressed, would have accelerated American Catholic life and progress by two full generations in the United States. Instead, in an illustration of how efficiently power may be used by men against men, Catholicism was sealed off from intellectual curiosity and was subjected instead to the rough and supposedly manly management of the Brick and Mortar era.

DUNWOODIE

Drawing on the talents of second-generation immigrants and converts to the Church, Catholicism in America evidenced healthy signs of intellectual curiosity and achievement during the second half of the nineteenth century. Nowhere were these advances better focused than at St. Joseph's Seminary, the training facility for the archdiocese of New York. Its century-old tower can still be seen from the parkways that twine around its location at Yonkers, less than an hour's drive north of Manhattan. Its distinguished faculty included priests well prepared in the new scriptural studies and theological investigations that had begun in Europe. Father Francis E. Gigot, then "the most advanced scripture scholar in America, set the tone in his 1900 article, 'The Study of Sacred Scripture in Theological Seminaries,' in which he wrote that 'the time is gone when the questions involved in the higher criticism might be simply

identified with rationalistic attacks upon the revealed word. . . .
One can no longer afford to be ignorant of topics which, perhaps
more than any other at present, engross the attention of the intellectual and religious world.' "²

.   These scholars found an extraordinary leader in Father James
F. Driscoll, a professor of Semitic languages, who was appointed
rector in 1902. He quickly transformed the formerly intellectually
sluggish and quasi-monastic routine of the seminary, assisted by a
team of forward-looking priest-scholars that included theologian
Francis P. Duffy, who would achieve fame a generation later as
chaplain of the Fighting Sixty-ninth, a heavily Irish American
World War I regiment.

Driscoll was convinced that priests should be educated on the
same level as other professionals. He scrapped the stodgy former
lecture series and invited noted scholars, Protestant and Catholic
(for example, Dr. Charles A. Briggs, president of New York's Union
Theological Seminary), to acquaint the students with the intellectual issues of the day. Driscoll also encouraged the students to take
additional courses at outside institutions and "with President
Nicholas Murray Butler and the Trustees of Columbia University
he negotiated an arrangement whereby Dunwoodie students were
accepted as graduate students. . . . and permitted to attend lectures,
at no tuition cost."³

The centerpiece of this ambitious intellectual revival was, however,
the founding of the first American theological journal, *The New
York Review* to be edited by Driscoll, assisted by Father Duffy and
philosophy professor Father John Brady. Its object, Driscoll wrote,
was "to discuss in a scholarly way, yet in a manner intelligible to
ordinarily cultured persons, lay or cleric, the various questions with
which the modern Christian . . . has to deal—mainly those per-
taining to Scripture and Philosophy."

He and Duffy proposed the project to New York archbishop
John M. Farley. "It was just what he wanted," Driscoll continued.

"He expressed his deep, long-standing regrets at the backwardness of Catholic writers in matters of modern scientific interest, and gave the opinion that it was due in great measure to the restrictive policy of the ecclesiastical authorities, who through their unreasonable methods of censorship (Index, etc.) only succeeded in stifling all initiative on the part of the ablest and best-disposed Catholic scholars."[4]

Farley wrote a supportive letter in which he assumed responsibility for the journal, and the first issue appeared as June–July 1905. It soon drew conservative criticism, and Driscoll had to defend it against charges in the Catholic *Boston Transcript* that it represented a "new, liberal Catholicism." "The purpose," he wrote, ". . . is not to abandon the old in favor of the new, but rather . . . to preserve with becoming care and reverence the old truths in the light of the new science."[5] As Gannon notes, "New York was opening its eyes and ears to the proclamation of truth in the natural, historical, and social sciences . . . promoting the study of theology and scripture in depth, in consort with the best minds in Europe. . . . And for all these reasons . . . [these advances] stood in an acutely vulnerable position as storm clouds boiled on the Atlantic horizon."[6]

INTELLECTUAL EUGENICS

The lightning strike came early in the summer of 1907 when the Holy Office issued a document, *Lamentabili Sane Exitu*, that proscribed sixty-five heretical propositions, most of which were taken from the work of the French scholar Alfred Loisy, whose student Driscoll had been at the Catholic Institute of Paris. On September 8 of that year, Pope Pius X, canonized half a century later, at the high point of the Brick and Mortar age, as a saint, condemned what he termed the errors of "Modernism" in an encyclical, *Pascendi Dominici Gregis*. In Gannon's apposite summary, these supposed "errors" included "most attempts then being made by European Catholics, priests and laity, to incorporate the most recent non-scholastic research into the development of theology and scripture studies. . . . [including] historical criticism, literary exegesis. . . . [and] cautioned against all systems of thought by whatever name which expounded on evolutionary theory of religion, or suggested that the Church reshaped external truths in every period of history according to its understanding, or otherwise threatened the validity and stability of dogma."[7]

The terrible swift sword of emasculation fell on the scholars as well as on their work. In various paragraphs, the Pope assailed their personalities and motivations, charging that "they play the double role of rationalist and Catholic . . . so craftily that they easily lead the unwary into error. . . . Audacity is their chief characteristic. . . . Well calculated to deceive souls . . . [they possess] the spirit of novelty. . . . It [the spirit of novelty] seeks to know beyond what it is meant to know, and . . . it thinks it can find the truth outside the Catholic Church, wherein truth is found without the slightest shadow of error."[8]

The objective of unmanning and humiliating these men was made clear. They were victims of "pride which puffs them up to vainglory," and the Pope charged bishops throughout the world that "it will be your first duty to resist such victims of pride, to employ them only in the lowest and obscurist offices."[9] In addition, "committees of vigilance were to be set up in each diocese for the purpose of detecting heresy; professors sympathetic to modernist views . . . were to be discharged 'without compunction'; books, periodicals, and newspapers . . . were to be subjected to the closest scrutiny and, where necessary, censorship; all further congresses of priests were prohibited, except on rare and prudently guarded occasions; and priests were forbidden to pursue studies in secular universities."[10]

In a document in November, the Pope declared as binding all past and future decisions of the Pontifical Biblical Commission, all but eliminating new scripture scholarship. Three years later he ordered that all candidates for the priesthood, all appointed bishops, and others take the Oath Against Modernism. It took several years for the full impact of this dramatic intervention in, and suspension of, Catholic intellectual life to be felt. When it came, it brought a blackout to the intellectual illumination that had occurred in such places as St. Joseph's Seminary.

At first, Archbishop Farley defended *The New York Review* from Roman criticism that was forwarded to him. In January 1908 the journal was, however, under a death sentence and was to appear only twice more before it was suppressed with a cover story that it lacked sufficient subscribers to continue. Archbishop Farley, Gannon suggests, had "developed a case of acute prudence" on the basis of informants in Rome who warned him about the dangers of modernism and for any archbishop to seem to be associated with any heresy. The journal died as the early darkness of anti-intellectualism fell; there would not be another American journal until the Jesuits founded *Theological Studies* in 1940. As Gannon makes clear, this was an episode filled with tale-bearing by ambitious clerics who wanted to be sure of their approval by Rome. In short, the use of power by men against other men.

REMEMBER THE *MAINE*

The climax for Dunwoodie did not arrive fully until the summer of 1909 when Farley, from Rome, cabled his vicar-general to dismiss Driscoll as seminary rector and to replace him, in as symbolic a gesture as the approaching era could possibly hope for, with Monsignor John P. Chidwick, pastor of St. Ambrose Church in Manhattan and the chaplain of the New York City Police Department. He had been on the battleship *Maine* when it blew up in Santiago Harbor in 1898, was accustomed to the parameters of institutional discipline, and immediately moved, as a man accustomed to carrying out orders would, to end the seminary's advanced intellectual program, which had come to be considered a romance with heresy. He stopped the students from attending Columbia University, for example, and in a melancholy footnote, the relationship withered until the Columbia trustees officially terminated it in 1925 because it had not been used in so many years. The new rector also decreed that all seminary classes be taught in Latin.

Driscoll was made a pastor, first of Chidwick's former parish in Manhattan and later in the town of Pelham in Westchester, where in 1923 he died, never having been allowed to return to his intellectual activities. He kept in touch with Charles A. Briggs of Union Theological and continued to attend in New York City gatherings of the scholarly group the Orientalist Society, to which he belonged, but his professional career lay in ruins. The official death certificate lists what is now understood as congestive heart failure as the cause of death, symbolic if not directly expressive of a broken heart.

Father Duffy left a year after Driscoll to become a pastor in the Bronx. If his intellectual career had been ended, he took up another as a hero army chaplain who earned overlapping but classic twentieth-century tributes. Pat O'Brien played him in the Warner Brothers movie *The Fighting 69th*, and a statue of him, in battlefield dress, now stands in what is known as Duffy Square, just above Times Square in Manhattan.

The eminent Chaldean scholar Gabriel Ousanni was forced to suspend his writing and was unable to continue his original research in the quarter century of teaching that remained for him.[11] The other scholars were also gradually dispersed as a new world order asserted itself in American seminary education. Students were not to be in or learn from the world; they were to avoid it and to sacrifice such intellectual curiosity or ability as they might have "for the good of the Church." As Gannon summarizes the results:

> *No cleric wanted to be counted part of a subversive*
> *company against* Mater Ecclesia, *and none wanted, by*

his writing or Instruction, to lead others into temptation.
Original research became original sin. The study of theol-
ogy became the study of approved manuals. . . . The
ordinary priest and the ordinary layman lapsed into
silence on matters bearing on doctrine. . . . The Ameri-
can clerical mind turned to . . . Gilbert Keith Chester-
ton's new book, Orthodoxy *(1908) and agreed . . .*
that, "if there is one class of men whom history has proved
especially and supremely capable of going quite wrong
in all directions, it is the class of highly intellectual
men." . . . The critical mind lay at ruinous discount.[12]

The brief candle of renewal at Dunwoodie guttered low and went
out. At least one observer grasped the dynamic beneath the
destruction of the spirit of freedom and learning that would not be
recovered in American seminaries until fifty years and more had
passed. Ironically, Vatican II would vindicate the vision and work
of men like Driscoll and Duffy. Gannon quotes E. E. Y. Hales, writing from that liberated perspective in 1964: "The price that has to
be paid when such high explosive is used can be tremendous; a kind
of intellectual *sterilization* may be included when thinking becomes
so dangerous [emphasis added]."[13]

DEPLOYING DEFENSES

As the power dynamic that squelched the Dunwoodie intellectual
revival could be identified as far back as Abelard and beyond, so it
beats a century later as a robust institutional pulse in Catholicism.
Those ecclesiastics of whatever rank who employ this tactic interpret it as a legitimate exercise or reclamation of the authority of the
Institutional Church. They bridle at dissent and reject, as inapplicable, unworthy, and unclean as biblical lepers any identification of
its possible sexual components. Such an interpretation is, to those

in whom these sexual filaments glow unmistakably, treated as subversive and dangerous, to be avoided, as random sexual thoughts should be, as occasions of grave sin. To suggest that eminent Churchmen might operate out of such complex sexual motivation is, in their classic line of defense, disloyalty to the Holy See and Holy Mother Church. These are not slight arguments, and they burden every intruder with feelings of guilt.

In order to understand how deeply ingrained are such responses, we should recognize them as psychological defenses, that is, arguments that are fashioned not for dialogue but to protect the self-image of those who experience the threat in such a diagnosis, no matter with what degree of sympathy it may be proposed. *Defensiveness* may, therefore, be listed as the common denominator of the use of power by men against other men. A psychological defense may be recognized because of its lack of emotional proportionality; its intensity and overinclusiveness betray it. A defense is powerfully functional, that is, it provides its users with an anaesthetic so that they do not feel the pain of the inconsistent position that it obscures. Perhaps most prominent of all, it justifies the opinions or actions of those who use them, making the rough ways smooth and assuring them that they are always right.

This defensiveness operates at the unconscious level, sealing the puncture in self-esteem that would otherwise occur so that the people thereby defended never even feel the blowout. Defenses also reveal our style and, to those who can read them, are filled with information about us. Defenses vary widely, according to their healthiness. Direct denial and fantasy are low-level defenses that point to the seriousness of the underlying personality problem. Others, such as the use of irony or humor, are high level and evince a healthy personality who knows how to dodge the slings and arrows of life without denying that they exist or that they themselves have some responsibility for their filling the air.

The pattern of defenses in the Dunwoodie suppression made room for neither irony or good humor. These self-insulating mechanisms were, instead, marked by denial and distortion; appeared to be motivated by fear, especially of loss of position or the esteem of superiors; and were directed not only at the rebuttal of intellectual arguments but at diminishing the persons involved by destroying their ability, or potency, to function. Thus, Fathers Driscoll and Duffy were made, suddenly and unconditionally, to surrender their capacity to think, conduct research, or publish. Their movement, as symbolized in the *New York Review,* was destroyed, as was the advanced theological and scriptural curriculum and their bridge to the modern world through their academic association with Columbia University.

Not only were the main characters made into non-persons, but the affair was also transformed into a non-event. Sometime during the generation following their deaths, almost all the records of that period in the history of St. Joseph's Seminary at Dunwoodie were removed from the archives or destroyed. In his 1928 book, *Catholicism and the American Mind,* Winfred Ernest Garrison, much as Hales would later, used a vocabulary that revealed these dynamics: "Catholicism today is less modern than it was a generation ago. . . . The liberalizing movements within the Church that were active thirty years ago have been either *crushed out or driven undercover* [emphasis add]."[14]

A long, dark anti-intellectual night descended on Dunwoodie and on American Catholic seminary education in general. It had been rendered intellectually docile and impotent. The future priest was to be a man after the early-twentieth-century masculine ideal: dutiful, athletic, uncomplaining, perhaps practical but hardly intellectual—a term that, applied to the priest in that period, was "a term of opprobrium."[15] Gannon cites the Brick and Mortar excuse of priests who explained that their lack of intellectual interest was a result of their being engaged in "practical" matters.[16]

We must recall that after the suppression of intellectual aspiration that had been diagnosed as "Modernism," priests found that "committees of vigilance" functioned everywhere to monitor their reading. The model for seminaries was thought to be that of West Point, with military-style training in which discipline and following orders were paramount. Patrick Cardinal Hayes succeeded Farley as archbishop of New York in 1919; his famous license plate, a capital H, bespoke his singular hierarchical grandeur. He appointed as seminary rector an elderly man with no academic experience. Hayes spoke of his priests explicitly as "soldiers of Christ" and revealed his attitude, demeaning beneath his gentle exterior, in the annual budget for the seminary library, five hundred dollars "for the purchasing, processing, and maintenance of books."[17]

Every priest in the world was required to take the celebrated Oath Against Modernism, and only forty felt free enough of the institution's control to refuse. Priest faculty members, such as those at the Catholic University of America, were expected to take this same oath at the opening mass of the school year until Vatican II.

This oath resurfaced at the installation ceremony of Father David M. O'Connell as president of the Catholic University of America on November 19, 1998, confounding many other leaders in Catholic education who were present. They were aware, however, that it was a signal about the bishops' intention to assert their control over the teaching of theology at Catholic universities. This movement, at the end of the century, was directly connected to the impulse for control that had unmanned the priest intellectuals at Dunwoodie at the century's beginning. This oath is only a symbol, of course, but it is not unfair to understand it as a loyalty oath as much as anything else, that is, the use of power by men over other men to re-enact a familiar myth in which seekers of the Grail are wounded in their manhood so that they can find no place of comfort for their painful and impotent state.

The ongoing assault on the intellectual integrity of priests reflects the magnitude of the threat that it has constituted for the institutional Church. This "no stone left upon a stone" approach may have an Old Testament resonance, but it sharply clashes with the teachings of Jesus or with the approach of the Catholic Church at its best, when it is pastoral rather than punitive in dealing with people.

One cannot easily dismiss the power, which echoes in these situations with unresolved psychological-developmental issues, of the "manipulative mother" defense, that is, the outright rejection of thinkers or their intellectual positions as insulting to the symbolic parentage of the Holy Father and Mother Church. Why, we must not only wonder but carefully and, indeed, respectfully ask, is this mode of relationship found so consistently in the institutional Church history of the past one hundred years? What lies behind this backbiting, rumor-mongering, condescending, humiliating, and shaming way of dealing with men and women, if not an uncreated and barely diagnosed sexual problem, an unhealed wound, we might say, that seems so threatened by health that it cannot bear and must overwhelm it?

Let us, undefended, examine these issues, defended still in the Church's institutional impulse to keep that wound from healing.

THE VARIETIES OF
ECCLESIASTICAL CONTROL

✝

"SO IT WAS BURNT. . . ."

I N THE TWELFTH CENTURY, in the person of Peter Abelard, we
meet "a Tristan of Brittany," as Joseph Campbell describes him,
richly gifted as a philosopher, theologian, poet, and musician, a
man who would ultimately be sexually maimed, but only after first
being brutalized by the Church for his leadership of the Scholastic
movement initiated by Anselm.[1] This system would be crowned by
the work of Thomas Aquinas and, almost eight hundred years later,
would be declared by the official Church as the only acceptable way
of thought in Catholic seminaries and universities.[2]

Abelard inspired fear in the official Church of his own time for
writing and teaching, as the Greeks had and Aquinas would, that a
knowledge of God could be gained by reason alone. This was in
response to the credo of unreasonableness expressed in the third
century by Tertullian, and quoted still today: "I believe because it is
absurd . . . the Son of God died . . . was buried and rose again; the
fact is certain because it is impossible."[3]

Abelard defended reasoning as a human experience that
implied "the reasonableness of God and that what reason cannot
accept, need not, and indeed cannot, be believed."[4] Thus, the doc-
tors of the Church should be read, "not with the necessity to
believe, but with the liberty to judge."[5]

This same Scholasticism that Abelard taught was sword and

shield for Pope Pius X when, a century ago, he led his war against Modernism that also destroyed, as if it were an innocent town in the wrong place, Catholic intellectual curiosity. That pope who would be made a saint by mid-century argued that "there is no surer sign that a man is tending to Modernism than when he begins to show his dislike for the scholastic method."[6] Abelard became, as many men and women have since, a hunted figure, "driven," as Campbell puts it, "throughout his mutilated life from one monastic haven to another. On one occasion he was compelled to burn his own work with his own hands."[7]

Abelard described this moment that symbolizes and recapitulates the sexual dynamics of subjugating, humiliating, and shaming. These may be identified, unchanged, a thousand years later in the official Church's dealing with those it judges to be dissidents: "So it was burnt amid general silence."[8] He was then required to read the Athanasian Creed, "which I read amid sobs and tears as well as I might."

Abelard was then sent to a religious house near Soissons, whose abbot Goeffrey maintained stern discipline by use of the whip, "from which he was presently released, only to fall into more trouble . . . until . . . he fled to a forest hermitage . . . to which . . . students flocked . . . from which he then took flight again for fear of the fierce power of . . . Saint Bernard of Clairvaux."[9] Abelard later wrote of despair so intense that he thought of going off to live a Christian's life in some non-Christian land. "Abelard was indeed Tristan as the mutilated Grail King, and he stands symbolic for his time and for the sterilization of heart, body, and mind that the Waste Land theme expresses."[10]

Abelard's life has been lived many times, its punishments and pain ever the same, and is being relived at this very moment, in the same brutal *pax de deux* between institutional Church and individual believer. In Abelard, then, we meet Everyperson, who, for trusting the truth of his or her own experience, has struck such fear in the hearts of the powerful that he or she must be brought under a control strong and smothering enough to destroy his or her potency. "Abelard," as we have read in Campbell, "had been the announcement, as in a symphony, of all the passages to follow, through which . . . the same dreadful murder of light and life by grim power (the art of the systematic exercise of power by men over men) was to be rehearsed."[11]

THOMAS MERTON

The features of this bitter imposition remain always the same. Even so great a spiritual master of our time as Thomas Merton re-enacted this scenario, unrecognized as such by us and perhaps not by him. In 1941 he had entered the Trappist Abbey of Gethsemani in Kentucky, the "strictest of the strict," as, without reluctance, it allowed itself to be called. The monastery, given to learning in previous ages, was a symbol, stark as a darkened cross, of the separation of mind and body, spirit and flesh, earth and heaven, that was its ascetic foundation. This was less a calling to become more human than to overcome being human at all. It represented a romantic absolute of rejecting the world, of ridding the intellect of its distractions so that it might find the Grail of union with God in contemplation.

Still, like many Catholics, especially clergy and professed religious, Merton found himself in the company of Abelard, entering the forest at its darkest part, leaving the common life of his abbey and the celebrity, not to say prosperity, he had brought to it, along with famous visitors and the world seeking his opinions. Merton is our Abelard as he moves into his "forest hermitage," where others—publishers and poets and that era's Vietnam War protestors—sought him out anyway.

There, seeking the silence free of the world's buzz, he would become what he considered himself at heart to be, a "solitary," tiring of others after an hour, or so he thought, as he mined the quiet of the woods for pure contemplation. Instead of leaving the human behind him and feeling well rid of it, he discovered the essential experience that he had lacked and, in his many self-images, had thought himself unfit ever to find: as he sought relief for one of his many wounds, after back surgery in a Louisville hospital, he fell in love, as men always do, unexpectedly and passionately, with a nurse who attended him there.

He had written about his "refusal of women" earlier in his life. Chastity was one thing, as he put it, but the lack of love he saw as his lot was quite another. He had not come to terms with the conviction that "man is most human, and most proves his humanity (I did not say his virility) by the quality of his relationship with women."[12]

He had, however, entered the field of transforming love for another human being, finding in that experience what he had never been able to will out of himself through monastic discipline or to think out of himself by intellectual effort. He had experienced what he had always doubted, what had been an abstraction in his relationship with God—that he was lovable, that a flesh-and-blood woman loved him as he was. As his biographer notes, "He loved greatly and was greatly loved. He was overwhelmed by the experience and it changed him forever. . . . Thomas Merton never again talked of his inability to love, or to be loved."[13]

Again like Abelard, Merton was tortured by great anguish as he suffered what all lovers must, the experience that cannot easily be divided, that must be taken as wholly as it takes men and women, knowing that it had touched something in him that he had sought to defend against or dismiss before. And Merton, trapped half by his fame and half by the monastery rules that he could not easily flout, saw the world bathed in a new light. Such love tutored Merton, as it does us all, in its fundamental truth: love does not divide but unites the personality, making its elements whole, integrating our sexuality, uniting and healing the wounds that our frailties and false knowledge leave in us.

Yet Merton was of the very institution that fostered such misunderstandings, and finally, as Abelard did with Heloise, he abandoned his beloved to her life as he became ever more estranged from his own. Abelard and Merton gaze at each other across the centuries, profoundly human, each a lyric-filled pilgrim on the same path. For they were both overwhelmed by love for a woman but finally undone by the emasculating institution that claimed them both for what was left of their lives. If this was the official Church rather than the mystical sacramental Church of which they had sung in their work, it was no less powerful as it broke them on the rack of love that was the truest thing in their lives, broke them as horses are broken, broke them on the institutional wall where hung the heads of heretics, that immense wall made for weeping that split intellect from emotions, spirit from flesh, soul from body.

WOUNDED FAREWELLS

Listen to their melancholy songs of farewell to the women who loved them and whom they loved—but not enough to break the Institution's deadman's grasp on them. They might both be responding from safe within the institutional fastness, their vows reclaimed as their loves were renounced, to the letter Heloise addressed to Abelard in the convent at Argenteuil, where she had gone at Abelard's urging ten years before:

> *Thou knowest, dearest—and who knows not?—how much I lost in thee, and that an infamous act of treachery robbed me of thee and of myself at once. . . . Love turned to madness and cut itself off from hope of that which alone it sought . . . Why, after our conversion, demanded by thyself, did I drop into oblivion, to be no more refreshed by speech of thine or letter? Tell me, I say, if you can, or I will say what I feel and what everyone suspects: desire rather than friendship drew you to me, lust*

*rather than love. So when desire ceased, whatever you
were manifesting for its sake likewise vanished. This, my
beloved, is not so much my opinion as the opinion of
all. . . . Listen, I beg of you, to what I ask, and it will
seem small and easy to you. Since I am cheated of your
presence, at least put vows in words, of which you have a
store, and so keep before me the sweetness of thine
image. . . . When little more than a girl I took the hard
vows of a nun, not from piety but at thy command. If I
merit nothing from you, how vain I deem my labor! I can
expect no reward from God, as I have done nothing out of
love of Him. . . . God knows, at your command I would
have followed or preceded you to fiery places. For my heart
is not with me, but with thee.[14]*

This voice of a woman is one to which the great institutions,
including the Institutional Church, have not easily listened out of
fear, perhaps, that the truth so truthfully demanded has seemed an
unbalancing and disorienting request. This is the voice of women
that men, fearful of what they might put at risk by replying in the
same spirit, have turned away from throughout history and that
they turn away from today.

The emasculating narrative takes the man back inside the
Institution, where, even though wounded and spent, he is approved
for putting aside what Merton's abbot, in the name of a thousand
bishops and religious superiors, transformed into the seductress by
referring to her as "the woman."

It is to this flesh-and-blood woman, demanding the truth about
their relationship, that Abelard, undone by her uncle's hirelings
and again by the Institution's men, replied in this way:

*I have composed a poem, which I send thee:
"O God, who formed woman from the side of a man
and didst sanction the sacrament of marriage; who didst*

bestow upon my frailty a cure for its incontinence; do not despise the prayers of the handmaid, and the prayers which I pour out for my sins and those of my dear one. Pardon our great crimes and may the enormity of our faults find the greatness of thy ineffable mercy. Punish the culprits in the present; spare, in the future. Thou hast joined us, Lord, and hast divided us, as it pleased Thee. Now complete most mercifully what thou hast begun in mercy; and those whom thou hast divided in this world, join eternally in heaven, thou who art our hope, our portion, our expectation, our consolation, Lord blessed forever. Amen." Farewell in Christ, spouse of Christ; in Christ farewell and in Christ live. Amen.[15]

This response to what really occurred with an abstraction denies and divides human experience so that what is natural is ever inferior to the separate and always more elevated level of what is supernatural. This dismissal of the loving Heloise by her beloved but unhealed, and perhaps beyond healing, Abelard has had parallels beyond counting. One in our own time is that by the love-tortured monk Thomas Merton of his beloved, known then and now only as "S."

As his biographer notes:

> *He had kept back the information [from his abbot] that he had left a love letter at the hospital and had made the first telephone call planning a meeting. This gave the impression S. had been the initiator. . . . There is a chilling passage in the journal: "If I drop her (and I suppose in a way I must—at least eventually) it must be gently and lovingly and not with pride (not seeking any kind of revenge! And not flatly and forever. . . .)." . . . What was most damaging of all, and something he was less aware of, was that he led S. on to feeling there was some*

possibility of his leaving Gethsemani to marry her. Then
he returned to his journal, both to write of the impossibil-
ity and to accuse S. of lack of understanding. . . .

When I got home, I called her and we were talking
again, foolishly, of possibilities, of living together, my leav-
ing here, 'marrying' her etc. But it is all preposterous. Soci-
ety has no place for us and I don't have the gall it takes to
fight the whole world particularly when I don't really want
married life anyway. I want the life I have vowed."[16]

One can mark the relationship's end in his final phone call to her,
or in his burning of her letters: "I did not even glance at any one of
them. High hot flames of the pine branches in the sun."[17] And yet
perhaps not its end, for the restlessness kindled by this human
experience had made a pilgrim of him for now, neither in
monastery or hermitage, could he find a place of comfort, and as
the king in our revelatory myth, he set out to find the Grail in a
non-Christian land, in the Orient, that world symbolic of Nature,
that Eden long abandoned by the West, a monk now who "talked
over and over of disappearing,"[18] whom no one could call back
from his intensely sought destiny.

Death kept its appointment with Merton in 1968 deep in the
Orient, on the far side of the world, near Bangkok, at a conference
on Eastern mysticism, in an accidental and mysterious electrocu-
tion that transfigured him in a flash of blinding and burning light,
marking him with the Grail King's wound, "a long raw burn mark
along the right side of his body almost to the groin."[19]

Both good men went to their graves with their unhealed
wounds left at the end by the Church that towered over their
monk-scholars' lives with no room for their yearnings to work and
to love outside its control. But they are only two among so many
who have found how wise in the ways of control is the Church as
an Institution, how powerfully its manipulation of sexual identity
and feelings has visited the suffering of Abelard and Merton on

millions, unnamed and unnoted. This use of power, largely by men over men, distorts and obscures what the Church as Mystery understands about human beings.

INSTITUTIONAL INSTINCTS

What needs exposure, again to sunlight and fresh air, is what transpires at the level of human experience, that hearth in which truth and love are fire-tried, what actually takes place in relationships rather than according to categories of the law. According to researcher A. W. Richard Sipe, "The current crisis involves the exposure of the structure that underlies a power system using celibacy for the domination and control of others."[20] What are the characteristics of this emasculating power that, with high refinement and averted eyes, visits inhumanity upon the human?

The Institutional Church allows itself to be as blind as the figure of Justice as it deals with individual men and women who, as Abelard and Merton before them, come to value the meaning yielded to them through their own direct human experience more than the interpretation forced on them by ecclesiastics. The first intuition, or reflex, of the institution is secrecy.

Ever and always, the transaction between the organization and the person must be hidden from view. Secrecy is invoked not so much to protect the privacy of the individuals but, beneath its cloak, to reinforce the power of the institutional arm as it strikes the blow. So secrecy serves control in official Catholicism; as in every institution, it is prized as an instrument of expediency and as a veil that blurs the goals of justice or truth. Secrecy is always a condition of its deliberations on human sexuality.

Perhaps the most famous recent example of secrecy in the service of control is found in the commission established by Pope John XXIII to study the issue of birth control in order to provide insight for the bishops convened in Vatican II. After his death in June

1963, his successor, Paul VI, continued the commission, enlarged its membership and its mandate, and tried to keep its existence a secret.

When news of its existence leaked out, he enjoined its members to follow strict secrecy in their convocations on a subject whose time, in view of the human experience of millions of Catholics, had come for open discussion. No minutes or other records would be published; neither would any photographs, professional or personal, be taken of the assembled group. Their work was to be delivered to Paul VI in secret and was to be used if and as he judged it to be acceptable. There is nothing particularly ecclesiastical or Catholic about exercising control through secrecy. Franklin D. Roosevelt, master of power as President of the United States, employed similar tactics, for if the report rendered in secret does not please the power that commissioned it, the findings can be ignored, their existence denied, and no oily furrow is left in the sea as a sign that the ship ever sank, much less sailed.

THE GOOD OF THE CHURCH

Paul VI may have been, as Garry Wills has observed, "a sincere believer, not a mere ecclesiastical politician . . . so convinced that Church leaders could not have erred that he hoped a broader look at the subject would end up confirming" the ban of birth control.[21] Despite the secrecy and the telling fact that married people eventually added to the commission were not, while in Rome, allowed to sleep in the same bed or even under the same roof together, the members raised serious questions about the rhythm method, previously advocated by Pope Pius XII, as no different in intention than artificial birth control and seriously disruptive of marital relationships already strained by the pressures of raising children.[22]

The commission discussions set off institutional alarms when twelve of its theologian members voted to change traditional

Church teaching and seven opposed it. Nine of twelve bishop members also voted for a change. Among the theologians was the American Jesuit John Ford, who had been placed on the commission at a late date and was to author the argument that finally prevailed. It is the institutional argument par excellence. The Church cannot, as an Institution, ever have been in error. To change this teaching now, no matter the human experience or sophisticated theological justification for doing so, would harm the institution and threaten its authority. The teaching must be sustained "for the good of the Church."

THE WOUNDED

The Pope tolerated the formation by Alfredo Cardinal Ottaviani, then head of the Holy Office, of a shadow commission whose members, including Ford, supported the institutional argument. Paul VI employed another Rooseveltian tactic in saying that despite the fact this was a rump ad hoc group and not the official commission, its dissent provided evidence that the commission members were divided on the matter.

The Pope was therefore shocked when, after issuing his famous encyclical, *Humanae Vitae*, in 1968, the human experience of Catholics authored a loud dissent and a readiness to follow the supremacy of conscience, another traditional Church teaching, in resolving the question of birth regulation. Indeed, in this effort to impose control for the sake of the Institution's consistency, Paul VI was himself wounded; in the ten years that remained of his papacy, he never wrote another encyclical. The Jesuit John Ford, along with other conservative theologians who proffered the institutional argument, had slain the heathen son of Nature as had the Grail King before him. Like the latter, Ford was also grievously wounded in his very potency as a teacher, and afterward he could find no place of healing or comfort. Back in the United States, he was rejected by the Jesuit seminarians, who refused to take his courses; his teaching career, cruelly counterpointed to Abelard's, was at an end.

The wounded were to be found throughout the world, victims primarily of the style of secrecy in exploring the subject that was, in fact, everybody's concern. This imposition of secrecy allowed the Institution to prevail even as it sustained a wound from which it is yet to recover. Fearing a loss of credibility, the fretting Pope chose to override the testimony of human experience in order to bolster the Church as an Institution. He and the Institution won, as the Grail King had, but were also disastrously wounded in their potency, in their ability to author statements on human sexuality that would be readily accepted by Catholics. This contrary outcome mocked the power it was meant to sustain and through which, in secret, it was forged. This also wounded the Church's genuine authority so that, as the millennium turned, the consciences of Catholics prevail over the pronouncements of the official Church in making decisions about their sexual lives.

STRATEGIES AND TACTICS

Sipe finds the strategy of institutional control implemented by numerous tactics, noting its expression in "the restriction or subjugation of the inferior group at the pleasure or for the use of the group in power. . . . There is no other way to phrase this reality accurately."[23] He identifies this subjugation in the sexual abuse of youth by priests, and of women by systematic degradation according to habits of thought and instincts so ingrained in many clerics that they do not even observe them.

This subjugation is pervasive but hardly subtle. It reveals itself as second nature in the classic clerical personality. Its first principle is that men are by God's design superior; every application follows easily from that, from the imbalance in the number of canonized males over females to the strenuous efforts and strained arguments to keep women out of the priesthood. The basic conviction follows the hierarchical model, at the top of which in the Church only a male may serve. He looks down, as kings once did by divine right, and understands better than those who are living them the lives of the men and women arrayed beneath him.

This confidence in the superiority of celibate male judgment in matters of human intimacy is withdrawn by ordinary people, and their willingness to accept subjugation overthrown, when these judgments do not match their own experience of love and sexuality. If, as Wills suggests, authority was a greater concern than sex to Pope Paul VI when he promulgated *Humanae Vitae,* "with John Paul, it is both *authority* and *sex* that are crucial. He fancies himself an expert, psychological as well as theological, on sex."[24]

JOHN PAUL II

Comes now John Paul, bearing the cross of the contradictions that are his as poet and priest, prey in himself to the mythical and the mystical in the Catholic tradition, anguishing over the world whose conflicts he recapitulates within himself. For one cannot but sense in him the elements that Hans Selye identified in stress, such as that associated with a wound: the *pathos,* or suffering, and the *ponos,* or toil, the work to overcome it.

It is interesting to note that although the Pope was a member of the commission of bishops that opted for a change in the Church's teaching on birth regulation, he found reasons not to attend the final meeting at which this vote was taken. In 1960 he had written a book, *Love and Responsibility,* whose opinions came from his discussions with young people in groups he had led as a priest. Now, as then, he strongly supports self-denial and the use of the rhythm method to regulate births.

As Pope, he has repeatedly and strongly supported *Humanae Vitae,* mentioning it, for example, more than forty times on a short trip to South Africa. He clearly views the West as decadent, identifying sexual immorality with the attack on the sacredness of life in abortion and birth control. John Paul II believes that he has brought insights into the nature of the person from his experience as a philosopher to this discussion. This sense of knowing better than his readers about sexual love comes across in his encyclical, *Familiaris Consortio*. It is also in this document that his commitment to a divided model of the person is evident and that his abstract celibate idealization of sex is prominent.

Thus he writes that "the innate language that expresses the total reciprocal self-giving of husband and wife is overlaid, through contraception, by an objectively contradictory language, namely that of not giving oneself totally to the other . . . the falsification of conjugal love."[25] This ideal is not, however, on the minds of most men and women, nor might it ever be, as they struggle to love each other as best they can beneath the ordinary burdens of life. It is beautiful, surely, but is clearly offered from a superior position, from a height that views the masses as living on an earthy plain far below, in a universe still divided into light and darkness.

John Paul is, however, consistent in maintaining a division to which he is so committed that he does not seem able to observe himself as he declares it. If sexuality is exalted, forgoing sexuality is exalted even more as he advocates abstinence as a good that equals and perhaps surpasses sexual union itself. Indeed, unless one is committed to this abstract ideal of refraining from sex within marriage, one may become the victim of concupiscence by engaging, or as rigorist commentators sometimes revealingly say, by "indulging" in it.

In a 1980 talk John Paul brings this abstract husband on stage, quoting Jesus [Matthew 5:28], "Everyone who looks at a woman lustfully has already committed adultery with her in his heart," and adding a new interpretation: "Christ did not stress that it is 'another man's wife' or a woman who is not his own wife, but says generically, a woman. . . . If (a man) looked in this way at the woman who is his wife, he could likewise commit adultery in his heart."[26]

Here, then, we find the point of inner conflict, the wound, if you will, against which the Pope struggles with little but brief abstract relief, the dangerous passion loosed in *Tristan and Isolde* that must be urgently tamed lest it overwhelm us, as the music did the audience on the night of its New York premiere. Indeed, the divided model of the person leads logically to this Armageddon between spirit and flesh in the heart of Christian marriage itself. The Pope, at great cost and great risk, is internally consistent as he implies that the ideal of virginal purity, of total chastity of intention and impulse, is, as the familiar phrase puts it, "the more perfect way" so that "freed from the constraint and from the impairment of the spirit that the lust of the flesh brings with it, the human being, male and female, finds himself mutually in the freedom of the gift."[27]

No knight has ever had a vision of love more pure, more impossibly romantic, or more tragically removed from the actual experience of ordinary human beings. At the same time John Paul II wrote these words, in the still-active skirmishes of the Sexual Revolution, many men and women, married and unmarried, found themselves oppressed less by the presence of passion than by its absence, plagued by an impotence that mocked the supposedly easy availability of sex and made them uncomfortable quasi-virgins.

Unwillingly, surely, John Paul does not heal, as he would, but rather reveals the wound, as he must, of a divided image of human beings. He is convinced that above the tumult of the world that he sees in thrall to lust, his voice proclaims the Gospel ideal by which he has lived. Yet this ideal of near angelic love lessens the value of love that is only human. One can almost see the energy rising like heat waves from John Paul's own muscular acts of the will to achieve and enhance his own celibate virginity and to advocate it as the-world-is-passing-away goal even for married couples.

This readiness to sacrifice the erotic is presented as mysterious and demanding and as divine in origin as Abraham's readiness to slay his son Isaac. John Paul II places this sexual offering at the heart of his vision of the mystery, emphasizing purity, even in the pure of heart, as ever and always referring to sexual purity. His elevation of the virginal undergirds his attitudes about marriage, celibacy for priests, his rejection of birth regulation except through the rhythm method, and his condemnation of any sexual expression, such as homosexual relations, that falls short of the conditions for "self-donation." This may mirror his own hard-won ascetic victories and his personal but remote mysticism that nonetheless remains outside the experience of ordinary people.

While respecting his own profound convictions, good Catholics must also search inside themselves to test where and whether this exaltation of the nonexpression of sexuality—this emasculation in the name of the Spirit—rings true in their own experience. They may also examine the arguments that are put forth to bolster what appear to be the Pope's own deep and guiding convictions about the issues in which he makes sexual abridgment an essential element.

Many critics of Vatican II argue that advocating such freedom to examine Church teachings to see if they fit or nourish human experience promotes what they deride as "cafeteria Catholicism," picking and choosing selections rather than accepting the whole menu as the rations for the Christian life. It is here that we pause to examine an ancient Church teaching whose relevance is as undeniable as its lack of use: the process through which a teaching, pronouncement, or practice is *received* and *accepted* by the ordinary believers who are expected to carry it out.

PART THREE

. . . . .

HEALING THE WOUND:
THE CHURCH AS MYSTERY

THE GIFT OF RECEPTION
IN CATHOLIC EXPERIENCE

✝

"HOW HIGH?"

D OWNSTREAM FROM THE SWELLS of the great Brick and
Mortar Age, an old image bobs on the surface of memory.
It is that of a once totally passive Catholic community
conditioned to receive and accept as God's will whatever the official Church bade its members to do. Only Buddhists could have
struck a more actively receptive style. Catholics lived at the bottom
of the great hierarchical triangle and were counted "good" if they
"knew their place" as subjects who, without murmur, embraced
their lot and, without question, accepted as true the teachings
handed down from the higher levels of the Church. Their role was
defined—as the strength of their faith was measured—by their willingness to receive whatever the Pope told them to believe, treating
doubts or wonders as mischievous distractions, if not outright sins.

This compliant spirit was sewn like a decorator's theme
throughout the fabric of life on the lowest level of the hierarchical
Church. So, in an ideal of that imperial period, the retreat master
would stand before an audience of priests and seminarians and proclaim the modal obedience of the era: "If the Holy Father commanded me to jump, my response would be 'How high?'" Indeed,
prominent among the virtues that were to be cultivated in the post-
Dunwoodie intellectual vacuum were obedience, docility, and the

willing acceptance of correction. This approach was in the service of absolute control of the Catholic conscience.

That this demand for almost trancelike acceptance was applied to such high-altitude abstractions as the doctrine of the Trinity was reflected in an ironic anecdote of the age. An old lady on her deathbed tells the priest come to anoint her, "True or false, I believe it all." Less often noted—for one was to banish such connections as in themselves sinful—is the resemblance between this expectation and the perpetual masculine fantasy of the controllable sexual partner who is nameless, faceless, uncomplaining, speechless to his ravishing, and ready to return for more. The controlled partner in such a sexual transaction has no desires or rights of her own, tells no tales, and lives, in effect, solely to satisfy the needs of the male, who is free of claims and exempt from giving anything back in return. This predator's daydream of open season on erotic indulgence is possible only if one can address the flesh without the spirit, depersonalizing the other by dividing her personality.

In that long Arctic twilight that spread over Catholic intellectual curiosity, the notion of the Catholic community's having any active role in forming or judging moral themes from their own experience was found only in vestigial phrases or structures or in old men's memories of life before Pius X's vigorous suppression of Modernism and its dangerous flirtation with independent thinking. Yet the community's role was encountered in such phrases as *Lex supplicandi, lex credendi*, which may be translated, "In what the people pray for, one finds what the Church believes." In moral-theology classes students learned that a safe basis for a moral choice may always be found in the convictions of the *sanior at maior pars fidelium*, that is, of "the majority of good healthy people."

RECEPTION BY THE COMMUNITY

Yet these were small memorial plaques to full personhood and the large truth about Catholics' active role and responsibility to transform the lightning bolts from on high into the spiritual and moral energy of life. Mentioned hurriedly, if at all, were the *munera*, or gifts, of the Church. Indeed, they are hardly, if ever, mentioned today. Nonetheless, one of the principal gifts is that of reception, a concept that indicates the positive engagement of the total Christian personality in assaying the truth and viability of the once force-fed formulas of Christianity.

Ancient and critical to the Church's understanding and integration of doctrines and practices, the practical meaning of the gift of reception flowers from the root, *recipere:* "to take in," "accept," "adopt." Recently, this concept has been treated by the Institutional Church as an embarrassing uncle shown up at the wedding without an invitation. The relationship is admitted, but he is regarded as out of place. Reception, however, is a thoroughly reputable concept that has always been understood as "a process whereby the faithful accept a teaching or decision of the Church; an ecclesial community or institution accepts . . . and makes this tradition or decision its own."[1]

A law may be passed or promulgated, but until it meets the test of community reception, it "does not as yet shape the life of the community."[2] As members of the community "encounter concrete, particular, and personal situations, they must come to a conscious decision to implement the law . . . The original norm of action meets the demands of real life and, as in a crucible, it reveals its suitability or its shortcomings."[3] The crucial role of human experience is thereby acknowledged. Finally, believers either affirm a teaching or practice "through steady observance, or [bring] to the legislator's notice the difficulties the law may generate . . . in the living spirit of *communio* . . . 'communion.' "[4]

Perhaps the first example of this active role of reception is found in "the recognition of the scriptural canon by Jews and Christians," how the books of the Old and New Testaments that are now considered the Canon of the Bible were so designated, and others put aside, on the basis of the community's careful sifting of them over time. The same notion of reception as a dynamic process of the believing community is found within the scriptures. Thus, Saint Paul "talks about teaching which he himself had 'received.' . . . Jesus speaks of the command he has received from the Father. . . . Receiving is the heart of New Testament soteriology [Christ's doctrine of salvation]."[5]

Even the decrees of some gatherings of the world's bishops failed this important test. As a result, there have been more coun- cils than received councils; as O'Donnell notes, the "reception of the seven great councils was not a matter merely of subsequent papal approval; more profoundly operative was the sense of faith whereby the bishops of the local Churches and their people wel- comed them into their liturgy and life."[6] This ancient tradition, therefore, recognizes the collegial, reflective, experiential testing of doctrines and practices as a true source of their validity. The acceptability of a doctrine is not—and never can be—its imposi- tion from the top, as if the Pope were sole master of interpreting and handing down what Catholics must believe. This gift acknowl- edges that the Spirit operates through local bishops and local churches and that the experience of ordinary people is crucial to any understanding of the Church's gift of reception.

Obedience can never be construed, therefore, as acquiescence in the mastery of another or as a literally mindless submission to another's control. People are violated when the price of their wor- thiness is the unconditional surrender of their God-given individu- ality and human capacities. What really takes place when any lawgiver invades human intimacy, whether priest or Playboy Advi- sor, if not something very like the male reverie of a costless sexual domination?

RECEPTION, YES, CAFETERIA CATHOLICISM, NO

It has long been accepted that the Spirit is heard in the voice of the community and its bishop; together, they affirm a doctrine by sift-ing the wheat from the weeds in order to harvest the healthy crop and burn the rest. This is a healthy expression of the believing community rather than an unhealthy subjugation to the unexam-ined and unhealthy demands of another.

The healthy community also speaks with quiet authority when it refuses to receive some teaching or practice. We may understand such sensitive community discernment as an accepted dynamic of the Spirit at work. It cannot be reduced and dismissed, as it is by critics of Vatican II, as a selective and self-indulgent picking and choosing of beliefs. The Church has always respected this process, as it did through the 1985 Roman Synod of bishops that was con-vened to reflect on "how Vatican II had been received in its four Constitutions."[7]

This sense of the believing community is, therefore, the com-mon sense of believers and has always been regarded, both in faith and morals, as a reliable guide to belief, decision, and action. The great Pope John XXIII, who convened Vatican II, found that the believing community may have loved him but could still intuitively refuse to accept his 1962 document, *Veterum Sapientiae*, decreeing that Latin should become the language of theological instruction in all seminaries. In recent history, however, nothing matches Pope Paul's encyclical *Humanae Vitae*, reaffirming the Church's long-term teaching against contraception, for its "virtual non-reception by many theologians and a large percentage of the laity in some countries."[8]

O'Donnell cautions that the reasons for rejection may be many, including the possibility that the teaching may be false in part or in whole or that it may be presented in a faulty manner or in language that makes reception very difficult. It may also be "mis-timed or mis-judged . . . [or] belong only to one era of the Church's life . . .

[or] finally, it may be misunderstanding, blindness, hardness of heart . . . that leads to non-reception."[9] Still, "serious questions must always be asked when there is non-reception."[10]

MEN, WOMEN, PRIESTHOOD

Indeed, serious questions have been asked by theologians and sincere Catholics about the official Church's position on almost all major questions of human sexuality. These are not the taunting questions of doubters or defamers but, for the most part, the sincere, conscience-driven inquiries of true believers. These have been daunting for Pope John Paul II, who, as we can see, is so personally committed to a singular ideal of self-oblation in matters sexual. He was therefore greatly troubled by the virtual non-reception of his brief letter of May 22, 1994, *Ordinatio Sacerdotalis*, by which he had intended to settle the question of women's ordination and to put an end to theological investigation and public reflection about this issue.

He wrote that "priestly ordination, which hands on the office entrusted by Christ to his apostles of teaching, sanctifying, and governing the faithful, has in the Catholic Church from the beginning always been reserved to men alone. . . . The non-admission of women to priestly ordination cannot mean that women are of lesser dignity, nor can it be construed as discrimination against them." Despite all this, he noted that "in some places it is nonetheless considered still open to debate. . . . In order that all doubt may be removed regarding a matter of great importance, a matter which pertains to the Church's divine constitution itself, in virtue of my ministry of confirming the brethren I declare that the Church has no authority whatsoever to confer priestly ordination on women, and that this judgment is to be definitively held by all the Church's faithful."[11]

A year later, one of the religious women who signed a letter appealing the decision to the Pope, Sister Carmel McEnroy, was fired from her teaching post in theology at St. Meinrad's Seminary in Indiana. This dismissal was widely regarded as the symbolic disciplinary response, a public lesson in what would happen to any theologian or group who tried to appeal the question in the future. It is no accident that the emblematic rejoinder from the Vatican was directed at a noncleric, a woman teaching in a man's domain who would not passively submit, would not fulfill the male fantasy by humiliating and surrendering herself without complaint.

THE USE OF FORCE

In October 1995 Joseph Cardinal Ratzinger attempted, allegedly at the Pope's urging, to bolt the door to this issue that could not be kept locked even with Peter's keys. Responding to an inquiry, Ratzinger maintained that the Pope's letter had been infallible, invoking the authority of his formal position as Prefect of the Congregation of the Doctrine of the Faith, thereby making *Ordinatio Sacerdotalis* as official and final a statement as possible: "This teaching requires definitive assent . . . since it has been set forth infallibly by the ordinary and universal Magisterium. . . . Thus, the Roman Pontiff . . . has handed on this teaching by a formal declaration, explicitly stating what is to be held always, everywhere, and by all, as belonging to the deposit of the faith."[12] In an accompanying letter, Ratzinger said that this would bring peace to people agitated by the question and that what the Pope had done was not to make the teaching against women's ordination infallible but to reiterate an infallibility it had always possessed as a doctrine of the Church.

Despite this retroactive massing of arguments and insistence on obedience, the question remains open. The community will not be passively compliant but will rather employ its gift of reception on an issue unmistakably steeped in the boiled-over issues of sex and gender. In June 1997, for example, the association of America's leading theologians, the Catholic Theological Society of America, by a vote of 216 to 22, with 10 abstentions, endorsed a paper that took issue with Ratzinger's position. This followed a similar position taken a year earlier by the Canon Law Society of England, which challenged the notion that excluding women from orders was an infallible teaching. Meanwhile, Cardinal Ratzinger, answering a press-conference question on whether Catholics made themselves heretics by advocating the ordination of women, said that they "support erroneous doctrine that is incompatible with the faith."

In July 1998 John Paul II issued a letter, *Ad Tuendam Fidem*, in which he bolstered his ban on women priests by adding, on his own, a buffer of penalties to canon law to be applied to dissenters from a newly designated class of infallible teachings, including that against women's ordination. In an accompanying commentary, Ratzinger added other examples of this new category of infallible teachings, such as the ban on euthanasia, prostitution, and, much to the discomfort of ecumenists, the invalidity of Anglican ordinations.[13]

Still, the discussion of the possibility of women's ordinations continues, as does a closer scrutiny of the arguments that have been raised against it and a deeper look at the early history of the Church. The Pope's teaching, which he has attempted to strengthen several times, has clearly not been received by a substantial number of Catholics or by a great many historians and theologians. These people cannot be derisively written off as "cafeteria Catholics" or be accused of chronically challenging the Pope out of some "spirit of disobedience" or "love for novelty," motives attributed a century ago to demean Modernists. Dissenters are dismissed as disloyal and as being agents, as Ratzinger sees it, of a corrupt secular culture that the Church must judge and from which it must remain aloof. Indeed, Ratzinger founds his position on a classically dualistic view of the cosmos and human personality, a divided universe and a divided person, the light of life and Grace ever threatened by the darkness of sin and evil.

Whose voice is here heard, that of the wild, untrustworthy world of Ratzinger's vision, or that of the believing community as it exercises its gift of reception by withholding its endorsement from a teaching that does not match its own experience? And if this is so, is there an unrecognized and surely unacknowledged sexual core to this rejection of a female priesthood, an unhealthy bias so ingrained as to seem natural to the clerical guardians of the all-male clergy?

This long-term defense now resembles a last-ditch effort by men acting somewhat like male golfers desperately worried that if women are allowed full membership in their club, they will invade their locker room and find them naked. Church officials surely seem equally unnerved and disproportionately anxious to keep women out of their lives and away from the priesthood. What conflict over gender are they coping with by an array of arguments that grows more brittle and less believable with every repetition? Is this labored effort less a crusade for theological truth, and more a way of adjusting to a deep and still painfully unhealed wound? Everyone in the Castle is saying exactly what the wounded Grail King wants to hear, yet he remains uncomforted and can find no rest, no ease, no peace, it would seem, because the poultices and penalties do not relieve but rather irritate an unnamed and unhealed wound.

GOOD REASONS, REAL REASONS

How can we suggest hidden motives, redolent of sexual conflict, beneath the arguments that Church officials offer against ordaining women? One does not plant the sexual element in these maneuvers, but one surely finds it there. The defensive quality of such pronouncements points to what is present but unacknowledged beneath the obvious impatience with the receiving Catholic community for not submitting totally to repeated and reinforced versions of the institutional teaching. While we must briefly survey some of the history of ecclesiastical attitudes toward women, our interest remains in understanding the unhealed sexual wound that throbs perceptibly beneath the surface of this discussion.

Even minds influenced by Ratzinger's operational vision of a divided and dangerous world cannot easily accept Pope Paul VI's arguments against women priests in his 1976 letter, *Inter Insigniores*. Looking away from what the Church's experience gave witness to then and proclaims even more clearly now—that most of the pastoral work of the Church is carried out by women—Paul asserts what John Paul II later endorses, that the Church cannot ordain women because Jesus called only men to be his apostles, that women cannot be priests because they do not look like men: "There would not be this natural resemblance which must exist between Christ and his minister if the role of Christ were not taken by a man. . . . It would be difficult to see the image of Christ. For Christ himself was and remains a man."[14]

This rationale and further argumentation, based on the priest as necessarily the groom to the bridegroom Church that relies on questionable interpretations of the Song of Songs, were put forward to support his decision, although somewhat tentatively, it is said, to lessen the possibility of confrontation with the Anglican Church, which had just allowed women to be ordained.[15]

These arguments were not convincing in and of themselves, and they were not and have not since been received by the Catholic community. Indeed, in the United States support for women priests rose 10 percent within two weeks of the issuance of *Inter Insigniores*.[16] Ten years later, two-thirds of Catholics approved of ordaining women. Polls, of course, do not decide Church teaching and may not fully reflect the "gift" of reception. However, their results do not argue against what ordinary people identify in their own experience about their readiness to acknowledge and accept women as ordained priests and pastors.

The fragile quality of the arguments against women priests suggests that they are kin to something with which we are ourselves familiar. We sometimes offer rationalizations to bolster our position when we cannot understand or admit the true inner reasons for our stance. Such rationalizations possess a pseudo-integrity: they are good reasons but are not the real reasons. Because these defenses are functions of our unconscious, we do not observe them directly, but others, however, catch sight of their patterns in our words, gestures, and attitudes.

The question then becomes quite different: what are the real reasons beneath these transparently weak arguments? What, we may legitimately ask when a papal statement does not ring true to us, is the real reason it was made? What is the false note that we pick up and to whose falsity we respond? The decisive argument for retaining the ban on birth control in *Humanae Vitae* was, as we have seen, not theological but institutional: if the Church is confronted with evidence of past misjudgment, it is threatened by the changes it must make if it admits a long, painful, and pain-inflicting error about human sexuality. A defense allows the institution to reject change and, at the same time, to maintain a consistent picture of itself. Thus, Paul VI's position against women priests, seconded and intensified by John Paul II, becomes increasingly less convincing as it becomes increasingly more defensive. Perhaps in no other area do we humans or our institutions more readily rationalize our opinions or behavior than in the sexual. It is preferable for many, including ourselves at times, to deny rather than to understand this human woundedness.

We protest too much, joining ourselves to that melancholy parade of people who are neither more nor less than human in their settling for weak explanations to avoid paying the strong cost of finding and facing the hard truths beneath their behavior. We turn away because these notions are inconsistent with our idea of ourselves, their potent truth threatens our long-established sense of ourselves. Were we to admit the truth without defenses, we would have to change ourselves. Some such process explains the official Church's protesting too much about its inability to ordain women to the priesthood. The official Church would have to change, an option that, as witnessed in the final institutional motivation for *Humanae Vitae*, it rejected as inconsistent with, because it is threatening to, its long-term sense of itself as incapable of error. As a result, the unhealed wound cannot be diagnosed for what it is— that which ails us—much less cured.

THE UNACKNOWLEDGED WOUND

In paragraph 6 of *Inter Insigniores*, Paul VI denies that the Institutional Church is influenced in rejecting women priests by its inheritance of the ancient opinions and rituals holding that women are intrinsically inferior to men and that their sexuality—full of danger, mystery, and blood—renders them impure and therefore unworthy to come close to the altar. The evidence suggests, however, that fear of and prejudice against women remain the powerful, if inadmissible, dynamics beneath the already weak arguments, made weaker still by the new canonical penalties attached to them, that rationalize an all-male priesthood as an eternal and undeniable divine decree—a truth, therefore, that lies deep in the nature of things.

Bad science makes worse theology, of course, and early errors about the nature of conception became compounded when Thomas Aquinas borrowed Aristotle's ideas to explain why women could not be ordained. He asserts that, in terms of the way nature operates, "a woman is an inferior and a mistake. . . . The male seed tries to produce something complete in itself, a male in gender. But when a female is produced, it is because the agent is thwarted, either because of the unsuitability of the receiving matter (of the mother) or because of some deforming interference, as from south winds that are too wet."[17]

It is not difficult, then, to understand why women cannot be priests: "Since any supremacy of rank cannot be expressed in the female sex, which has the status of an inferior, that sex cannot receive ordination."[18] This gave some legitimacy to the many statements of early Church fathers and later theologians about the evil and seductive qualities of women. These include Duns Scotus's claim that because women are the daughters of Eve, who brought about man's fall, they cannot be instruments of man's salvation. Tertullian described women as "the gateway through which the devil comes." Albert the Great, Aquinas's teacher and the father of Scholasticism, argued that "woman is a misbegotten man and has a frailty and defective nature in comparison with his. Therefore she is unsure in herself. What she herself cannot get she seeks to obtain through lying and diabolical deceptions. . . . One must be on guard with every woman, as if she were a poisonous snake and the horned devil."[19]

The taboos against women at or near the altar can, however, be traced to the complex of regulations related to Jewish temple worship. Women were thought to be impure because of menstruation and childbirth and, indeed, impure for twice as many days, sixty-six, after bearing a girl than after bearing a boy, thirty-three (Lev. 12: 1–5). Women were kept at a distance from the altar, behind screens. Such attitudes were transferred to the early Church, in which women, who had been easily and fully accepted by Jesus, were gradually exiled from his holy places by various councils, decrees, and practices. Well within the memory of older Catholics is the scene of a new mother kneeling at the altar rail being "churched" by a priest, assisted by an altar boy. This postpartum purification held, as clearly as a tissue sample does, every fear, suspicion, and superstition about women that lingered on in the Church. Deep in the triumphant times of Brick and Mortar, the newly compiled Code of Canon Law stated flatly that "female persons may in no case come to the altar, and may give responses only from afar."[20]

Are we surprised to discover the complicated sexual roots of denying women any access to the choir space in church? As a result, only men were allowed to sing in Catholic choirs, witnessed in the gracious ebb and flow of Gregorian chant made as much for male voices as the songs of Welsh miners. This exclusion of women, however, led to the perversity of the castrati, emasculation in the service of the institution, in which the soprano voices of boys were guaranteed by surgery that, as in every use of emasculation, unmanned them, subordinating their potency to an institutional need that lingered in Rome itself until the twentieth century. That castrating children was thought morally preferable to allowing women to sing in the choir is perhaps the clearest sign we have yet come upon of how long the sexual wound in the official Church has been denied and gone unhealed even as it motivated bizarre, highly rationalized perversity.

DID AN ALL-MALE PRIESTHOOD EVER EXIST?

Both Paul VI and John Paul II insist that Jesus established an exclusively male priesthood, that they are only retelling the tale of New Testament times to guarantee the purity, consistency, and integrity of Church understanding and practice. Read the New Testament, they say, and learn that God decreed the exclusively male priesthood and that we lack the authority to change this truth. Women, whom we honor in so many other ways, must simply adjust to this reality.

In fact, however, such argumentation is in itself questionable in the light of the scriptural scholarship that (after the long dark night of imposed impotence that followed the unforgiving suppression of Modernism) has revived and allowed us to revisit the early Church. There we find a very different understanding of priesthood and of the role of women in the Church than that offered by recent popes. So great and faithful a scripture scholar as the late Raymond Brown places the right question: "Did the historical Jesus think about ordination?"[21]

He answers that "there is no biblical evidence that he thought about any of his followers, male or female, as priests, since there were already priests in Israel. . . . From the New Testament it appears that the clear conceptualization of the Christian priesthood came only after the destruction of the Jerusalem Temple in A.D. 70."[22] The papal arguments that Jesus chose the first priests without including a woman, not even his mother, cannot easily be sustained, much less ever validated by reception by the believing community, because, in the first light of the Church's founding, Jesus appointed neither men nor women to the priesthood.

THE WAY WE WERE

Indeed, biblical scholars also reveal the general life of the early Church in which women played significant roles equal to and in the company of the earliest apostles. As summarized by Uta Rank-Heinemann:

> At first women were actively involved in the expansion of the young Church. Paul reports (1 Cor. 11, 5) that women preached during the liturgy just as men did. He speaks of women's "prophesying," which means an act of official proclamation, best translated as "preaching." Women such as Phoebe were deacons (Rom. 16:1–2). Paul also calls himself the deacon, or minister, of a community (Col. 1:25); and part of the service rendered by the deacons was teaching (Col. 1–28). In the letter to the Romans (16:3) Prisca is called a "fellow worker in Christ Jesus," a term that for Paul always carries with it a special authority. Service in the Church is characterized in 1 Corinthians 16:16 as "working hard."
>
> In Romans 16:12 three women, Tryphaena, Tryphosa,

and Persis are described as "working hard in the Lord."
And in First Thessalonians (5:12) people who do such
work are equated with "those who are over you."[23]

The gradual degrading of women's roles, including changing the name of Junia, a woman characterized by Paul as "outstanding among the apostles" (Rom. 16:7), to the safely male Junius, was not the work of Jesus nor the practice of the early Church. Indeed, as French Dominican theologian Yves Congar, raised to the cardinalate by John Paul II to redress the ecclesiastical suppression of his work in the 1950s, has observed, one cannot find ritual priesthood in the New Testament.

"The word *hiereus* [priest, sacrificer] appears more than thirty times in the New Testament, and the word *archiereus* more than one hundred and thirty times. . . . It clearly shows a deliberate and highly significant intention, especially as the writers of the first Christian generation very carefully follow the same general line. With them, as with the New Testament, *hiereus* (or *archiereus*) is used to denote either the priests of the levitical order or the pagan priests. Applied to the Christian religion, the word *hiereus* is used only in speaking of Christ or of the faithful. It is never applied to the ministers of the Church's hierarchy."[24]

We have identified the stirrings of truth in that vasty deep in which the powerful currents of truth so fully flood the sea that they seem neither to move nor be moved, and time is of no account. These are the waters of the Church's unconscious, that realm in which every transaction is recorded as it is, not as it is made to seem in daylight consciousness. Churchmen who trim their sails to catch the ever changing surface winds may preach of eternity, but they serve time as their master. So they choose the literal over the metaphorical, the temporal over the eternal, the simplicity of the proof text over the complexity of the truth itself.

Thus, they often misread and misapply Jesus' phrases as they pluck out their eye of understanding rather than see into the sexual nature of their habitual surrender to institutional need. A sense of self-righteousness, of orthodoxy restored, supports their foreshortened view of the arguments that are still used to suppress women and to glorify virginity as the most perfect of all choices. As long as they catch the passing wind, they feel that they are sailing the approved course, that by thus pleasing him they will win the approval of the Master of all fleets. Not for them the darkest part of the woods or the deepest part of the waters. Yet they are good men in their way, builders of the breakwater against the authority of the sea, saviors, as they see it, of the sheltering harbor rather than searchers of the treasure-laden waters.

Is it not best, they ask, to choose the safest course even if the outdated maps yield no true reading? To them, that justifies their acceptance of arguments that are massively inadequate—theologically, scripturally, and psychologically—on the central questions of human intimacy. What process allows or commands them to do this?

They re-enact before our eyes the profound mythic theme of sexual wounding, of their determination to overcome Nature, of their raising their lance against this heathen rider from the East, of killing yet being wounded by him in the encounter, of suffering a sexual wound by their mighty effort to kill all that is natural and human. A victory mythic and Pyrrhic, at a price never paid in full but exacted every day. They thereby make themselves eunuchs for the sake not of the Kingdom but of the Institution, sacrificing their intellectual potency and vigor, submitting to the chronic humiliation that is the scalding feature of the use of power by men over other men.

Beneath their denials and distortions, we catch a glimpse of the unhealed sexual wound in institutional Catholicism, for it is borne not in the abstract but in real life. We enter again that Grail Castle in which the bent and fevered King can find no rest and in which the courtiers are too intimidated, too fearful of losing everything, too wounded themselves, to ask Parzival's simple human question, What is it that ails you?

The stakes are by no means small, because such officials have wagered heavily on their claim against women priests, insisting, for example, that the exclusively male priesthood and bishopric can be traced directly to the mind and words of Jesus. Yet this is not—and has not been for some time—supported by the scriptures or theology. Yet the immediate reward of a sense of control must exceed the deferred pain of the losses suffered because of their misreading of scripture, theology, and human experience. The time-ridden official Church ranks as acceptable casualties those killed or missing in this action that the Church as Mystery would never allow. Institutional leaders even accept a loss of sacrament to the faithful as preferable to accepting women or married men as priests to preside at the Eucharist. They would rather look away from than identify and heal the sexual wound from which the Institution so suffers that it interferes with its proclamation of the Church as Mystery.

Let us look more closely at the dynamics beneath this emasculation of the self in the name of celibacy and virginity, this submission that delivers unconscious sexual gratification as a reward for rejecting conscious sexual gratification.

MAIMED FOR THE KINGDOM

✝

B OTH POPE PAUL VI and Pope John Paul II have not only defended celibacy as a requirement for the priesthood but also removed it as a subject of discussion by the world's bishops, the only body with the competence and the obligation to explore its meaning, derivation, and real-life condition. Pope Paul VI made a preemptive strike during Vatican II in an intervention that remains, these long years later, as astounding as it is defensive.

If Paul VI made what can hardly be termed a collegial intervention on celibacy, John Paul II has seconded and raised his predecessor's conclusions to another power. These papal interpolations share an undisguised purpose—to take control of the discussion of celibacy through invoking papal authority, to bet on it, in a sense, as an ultimate and unanswerable test of Catholic loyalty and readiness to yield in the matter. However, these statements also exemplify the use of power by men over other men. If we clip away the impressive ecclesiastical seals and signatures, we may identify their shared dynamic of the active assertion of complete dominion over other men through controlling their sexuality.

The need to master other men—to keep them unmarried and in exile from intimacy with women—may then be understood as their virtual emasculation "for the good of the Church," disguised, through now untenable scriptural arguments, as celibacy "for the sake of the Kingdom." The lack of proportion between the demand that celibacy remain unquestioned, even by the bishops of the

Church, and the disappointingly weak scriptural arguments offered to support it suggest a frayed glove accentuating rather than hiding the iron hand of force.

These directives come from men with institutional concerns. They are restless and anxious about their capacity to carry out what they believe to be their right and their duty, to justify the Church's long season of obsession with human sexuality by reinforcing control over it in the lives of the only persons the Church can control, the priests. Despite their avowals of commitment to the dignity of the abstract person, neither Paul or John Paul has made his peace with real people. That these pontiffs have operated from a divided model of men and women is evident in their judgments that sin and virtue depend on the opposition of spirit and flesh, soul and body, unviolated purity ever imperiled by the surges of carnal sexuality.

OBSTA PRINCIPIIS: RESIST BEGINNINGS

In the practical use of power, the best way to stop a discussion is to keep it from starting. Learning that some bishops wanted to discuss celibacy on the floor at the council, Paul VI sent a letter to the assembled bishops, in which he announced that "without infringing in any way on the right of the Fathers to express themselves, we make known to you our personal opinion which is, that it is not opportune to have a public discussion of the topic, which demands so much prudence and is so important. We not only intend to maintain this ancient, holy and providential law to the extent of our ability, but also to reinforce its observance, calling on all priests of the Latin Church to recognize anew the causes and reasons why this law must be considered most appropriate today, especially today. . . . If any Father wishes to speak about this matter, he may do so in writing by submitting his observations to the Council Presidency which will transmit them to us."[1]

In an extraordinary elaboration on this unilateral action that effectively rendered impotent the only men who, gathered together, could discuss celibacy in a meaningful way, a papal aide, Monsignor Paul Poupard, explained that the Pope acted, in a word brimming with revelation, out of *"fear* of allowing the public appearance of division . . . and also the *fear* that, in view of the pressure of the mass media, [the council fathers'] interventions on the subject *would not be free* [emphasis added]."[2] In fact, it was Paul VI who guaranteed that neither they nor their discussion would be free. Apparently concerned that the world's bishops might attempt diagnosis and treatment of this unhealed sexual wound, Paul VI judged it to be inoperable, sewed up the incision, and sent the patient back to his uncomfortable existence. There would be no exploration of what the experience of mandated celibacy is actually like in priests' lives.

Paul and John Paul after him have not been nearly as interested in celibacy in itself as in keeping the authority of the Institutional Church—and their own—from fragmenting under the impact of the force five winds that would be unbound by an open discussion of a largely hidden problem. The ever anguished Paul was afraid, in the sentiment accurately if unconsciously attributed to him by his surrogate Poupard, of the institutional consequences of surrendering his control of a discussion that, unrestrained, would lay bare the unhealed wound of sexuality in the official Church. Paul VI's distress seeps through like blood on a bandage in his lack of ease in managing this wound. He is truly the Grail King, for he is painfully aware, as John Paul is not, of his own incapacitating discomfort because he fears the consequences for the institution of free discussion. Thus, Poupard's rationalization, since perfected in other settings, of blaming the media for the Pope's own action of abridging the bishops' freedom to discuss the subject.

THE ENCYCLICAL THAT DID NOT HEAL

In June 1967 Paul VI followed up his intervention in the council with an encyclical, *Sacerdotalis Caelibatus* ("Priestly Celibacy"). The Pope was forced to meet institutional ends rather than human needs in a document that not only failed to match the celibate experience of priests but repeated biblical arguments that, after the recovery of biblical scholarship in the Church at mid-century, were recognized as literalistic "proof texts" at best and inappropriate and irrelevant at worst.

Then and now, the way priests actually practice celibacy varies considerably in the Catholic world. In general, North American priests have always so striven for a bewildered and bewildering observance that they were described in a dismissive Italian clerical joke as *scrupulosi Americani* (scrupulous Americans), that is, taking the rules far more seriously than their colleagues in Latin climes. It has been no secret that in those countries, it has not been unusual to find priests living openly with mistresses or with wives and children in a custom so long accepted as to defy modulation, much less reform. In Africa the Western notions of monogamy and celibacy have been foreign to the experience of the people; the great German theologian Karl Rahner, among others, felt that the Church would not betray its mission by reconsidering its moral theology in respect to well-established non-Roman courtship and marriage traditions."[3]

In Western countries, during and after the council, priests had not only asked for an examination of the requirement of celibacy but, in numbers in the thousands, had begun petitioning to be relieved of their obligation of celibacy in order to marry. Although Paul said that these men would not have departed "if they knew how much sorrow, dishonor and unrest they bring to the Holy Church of God," he also liberalized the process, later closed down by John Paul II, of allowing men to withdraw from the priesthood, "thus," as he said, "letting love conquer sorrow."[4]

However, he saw no way of changing the celibacy requirement without visiting chaos on the Church as an Institution. Despite the paeans to celibacy as the ideal state for the priest as servant to the community and as a privileged and blessed calling to a higher life, studies have revealed that most priests have not found such spiritual satisfactions in celibacy but, in diverse ways, ranging from isolating hobbies to the faux camaraderie of golf, adjust to not being married.

Neither did the encyclical address or even acknowledge the hidden costs of celibacy in the widespread sexual conflicts and problems that, as in other great organizations, were managed discreetly to minimize public notice and to maintain the surface appearance of organizational integrity. This also prevented, as it would a dozen years later when the crisis of priestly pedophilia finally broke open, any continuing scientific research into the sexual maturity or adjustments of priests. This extensive defensiveness signaled an awareness of a wound that, from the institutional viewpoint, was better denied than described and treated.

Indeed, the cardinal archbishop of Philadelphia, John Krol, chair of the bishops' committee for the multidisciplinary studies of the priesthood (1969–71), argued vehemently against researchers asking *any* questions or soliciting *any* information about the sexual behavior of priests, claiming that it was a matter for the "internal forum," the confidential enclosure of the confessional. Long before the U.S. Armed Forces, the official Church sponsored a "Don't ask, don't tell" policy regarding the sexual behavior of priests. They would rather not look at the wound than admit either that it existed or their inability to heal it. This did not deter the investigators from examining the real-life conditions of celibacy.

THE PROOF TEXTS

The exaltation of virginity for Christians in general and of celibacy for priests and professed religious, in particular, has long been based on the scriptural texts on which Paul VI raised his argument in *Sacerdotalis Caelibatus*. Pope John Paul II has also championed clerical celibacy, making a record of absolute loyalty to it an essential requirement in any man he has appointed a bishop. In his 1979 "Letter to All Priests of the Church," he uses the same texts that Paul had employed. These alleged scriptural foundations for celibacy have also been cited in documents and ascetic tracts beyond number.

The great justifying theme of all of these is found in Matthew 19:3–13:

> And there came to him some Pharisees, testing him, and saying, "Is it lawful for a man to put away his wife for any cause?" But he answered and said to them, "Have you not read that the Creator, from the beginning, made them male and female, and said, for this cause a man shall leave his mother and father, and cleave to his wife, and the two shall become one flesh? Therefore, now they are no longer two, but one flesh. What, therefore, God has joined together, let no man put asunder." They said to him, "Why, then, did Moses command to give a written notice of dismissal, and to put her away?"
>
> He said to them, "Because Moses, by reason of the hardness of your heart, permitted you to put away your wives; but it was not so from the beginning. And I say to you, that whoever puts away his wife and marries another, commits adultery, and he who marries a woman who has been put away commits adultery." His disciples said to him, "If the case of a man with his wife is so, it is not expedient to marry." And he said, "Not all can accept this teaching; but those to whom it has been given. For there are eunuchs who have made themselves so for the sake of the kingdom of heaven. Let him accept it who can.[5]

Although this paragraph has been trimmed and braced to support celibacy, even the nonscholar can see that Jesus has not been asked about celibacy but rather, by the Pharisees, about divorce. He answers with a statement truly revolutionary for those times, when men were allowed to divorce spouses easily for even trivial reasons, such as household foibles or preparing meals poorly. Jesus' words remain startling in the era of no-fault divorce. Women had no reciprocal right, as they were considered the property of their husbands.

Jesus says that if a man divorces his wife to marry another woman, he thereby commits adultery. This is a hard saying for even his closest followers to accept. To them, Jesus replies that not every man can receive this saying and continues, using a metaphor of self-castration for the Kingdom of Heaven, to dramatize the extraordinary demand made on the man who puts aside his wife.

Castration is here a metaphor, one commonplace in the mythopoetic language of the scriptures, and cannot be understood as a concrete literalism. The metaphor clearly refers back to the dialogue about divorce. Through its use, Jesus describes the radical nature of the voluntary renunciation of adulterous remarriage. It does not refer to celibacy, as commentators point out, but to Jesus' repudiation of adultery and divorce. There is a curious modern aura to the reaction of the disciples who were themselves married. If this is the law, they ask, then wouldn't it be better to live with a woman without marrying her? The ideal they find hard to accept is the fidelity that binds a man as much as a woman in a permanent, unbreakable marriage bond. To this, Jesus responds, "Let him accept it who can."

Jesus then, as Jesus now, startles the complacent world with this unambiguous rejection of adultery and divorce. Even employing an interpretation as artful as the late Supreme Court Justice William O. Douglas's sensing of hints and "emanations" about the right of privacy in the U.S. Constitution, one cannot interpret Jesus' words as a command that his married companions be celibate. Yet Paul VI cites these words four times as the foundation for his defense of celibacy, and John Paul II invokes this passage again in his efforts to infuse celibacy with a divine origin and some immediate and necessary connection with a priesthood that, at the time of Jesus' statements, had not yet entered the imagination of the infant Church.

INSTITUTIONALIZED DESEXUALIZATION

John Paul II comes near to absolutizing celibacy by referring to it as "apostolic doctrine."[6] This clashes with what the apostle Paul identifies as the right of the earliest followers of Jesus—the apostles in whose number we find the first pope, Saint Peter—to be accompanied by their wives on their journeys: "Don't we have the right to be accompanied by a sister [a Christian woman] as a wife, as the other apostles and brothers of the Lord and Cephas [Peter]?" (1 Cor. 9:5).

This statement was gradually changed in later translations that transformed *wife* into *woman* and rearranged the phrase so that "a sister as a woman" became "a woman as a sister," eliminating the idea of marriage altogether. This reading was confirmed, against the evidence of twenty-eight Vulgate readings with the correct sense, by the Clementine Vulgate of 1592 that became the official edition of the Latin Bible. So, too, by the second century, the "brothers and sisters of Jesus" mentioned in Mark 6:3 and in Matthew 13:55 became "step-brothers and step-sisters" and by the fifth century are male and female "cousins."[7]

Paul's statements in First Corinthians expressing his wish that the unmarried remain so as he himself was, has also been used to support virginity and celibacy as higher callings than marriage. The apostle later insists on an apostle's right to marry, speaking in such a qualified manner that even an untutored and unsophisticated reading of his words hardly yields a definitive anti-marriage, pro-celibacy interpretation. Paul speaks from a context difficult for us to understand because our acquaintanceship with an urgent sense of apocalypse is limited to the eccentric communities who periodically head for shelter to await together the imminent end of the world. In the first century there was a generalized expectation about Jesus' return that was of a more solemn and less hysterical character.

Even from this perspective, Paul offers diffidently and almost apologetically observations that he wants not to be taken as anything more than opinions: "I give this as a recommendation, not a directive: I prefer that all men be as I am. But each has his own spiritual gift from God, so one will act this way, another that way (7:6–7). . . . This is I speaking, not the Lord (7:12). . . . I have received from the Lord no requirement concerning virgins, but I offer my opinion as one in a position of trust (7:25). . . . I say this for your benefit, not to tie you in a rope (7:35). . . . This is just my opinion . . . (8:40)."

MYTHS AND METAPHORS

One of the extraordinary aspects of the defense and promotion of clerical celibacy is the passion with which both Pope Paul VI and Pope John Paul II have invested their arguments. They resemble lecturers with their heads lowered to their yellowed notes against the possibility that a bright student might raise his or her hand and ask a hard question. This may reflect, as it would surely seem to with John Paul II, the emotional overflow of his own strenuous pursuit of this celibate ideal. Paul VI's passion is more that of an artist overwhelmed by his keen vision of the institutional circumstances he must mediate and bring into balance. Their feelings, raised exponentially by their sense of responsibility for maintaining papal authority and institutional integrity, may have urged them to read the scriptural bases for celibacy in a concrete and literal fashion. However, this is to use force against the truth in order to use the resulting distortion against men and women.

This concrete reading of the scriptures snuffs the life out of their words as repositories, movable feasts in a real sense, of mythological and metaphorical meaning. Only an appreciation of the latter can deliver their authentic "spiritual" meaning. The language of religious mystery is also that of mature spirituality but is not to be confused with that of the almanacs or newspapers, which presume a generalized understanding of metaphor when they run leads such as "The roof blew off the Trenton courthouse today in the Lindbergh kidnapping trial." This does not report or refer to a damaged civic building but to the intensity of the exchanges on one day at a trial that mesmerized the nation in 1935. "David slays Goliath" on the sports page is not read as a news flash from Jewish history but as a way of saying that an underrated opponent beat an overconfident first-place team.

Enormous problems for religion—and for human sexuality—have arisen because of the confounding of the language of metaphor with the language of fact. Indeed, religion and human sexuality overlap because they are so profoundly human that they speak the same language. It is not unusual to encounter metaphors from the one used to describe the other. Many dimensions and conditions of sexuality have been described in spiritual metaphors, and many spiritual experiences have been described in sexual metaphors. The failure to understand the meaning and use of metaphor in human communication has caused enormous pain to human beings. It is one of the reasons that the sexual wound is so poorly diagnosed and has been so hard to heal.

THE METAPHOR OF VIRGINITY

We may better distinguish the Institutional Church from the Church as Mystery in the way they read and integrate within themselves the metaphorical language of myth and religion. The Institutional Church examines a metaphor and takes it literally, that is, in its *denotative* or concrete sense. The Church as Mystery, as a People of God, reads a metaphor in its *connotative* or psychological and spiritual sense. The Institutional Church manages facts: the casings of life in times and places, dates and sums, the physical evidence before the eye. The Church as a people shepherds mystery: the interior life in the flow of spiritual insight and revelation, the evidence beyond the eye.

Perhaps nothing has more confused the meaning of religion and our understanding of human sexuality than confounding the denotative, or literal, meaning with the connotative, or spiritual, meaning of metaphor. Metaphor has always been an abused concept and is no less so at the beginning of the third millennium, when popular political and social commentary chronically debases the notion by equating it with *symbol*, as in "The Lewinsky affair is a metaphor for the Clinton presidency."[8]

Misreading metaphor as essentially concrete and time-bound rather than spiritual and transcendent of time has caused enormous difficulty in the understanding and practice of religion. While it is easy to recognize the fundamentalist reading of the "end of the world" metaphor as a scenario for the concrete, cataclysmic ending of sinners and a sinful earth, one seldom hears its spiritual meaning evoked, even though this richer meaning opens the individual to the transcendent. In the connotative, spiritual meaning, the end of the world occurs every day or whenever we can see into the mystery of creation. At that moment, the world, whose surface we have not penetrated because we have focused too closely on it, comes to an end.

For our reflection, we summon up another metaphor, the unhealed wound that pervades so many mythic stories, that mystery not of a literal wound but of our spiritual distress at the violent division of flesh and spirit that has shattered our sense of, or hopes to attain, a unified self. Perhaps no metaphor has been more often misunderstood and misappropriated than that of the Virgin Birth. Like the end of the world, it connotes a spiritual, transcendent reality rather than a physical, historical event. This misreading of the concept of the Virgin Birth has been responsible for much of the

Church's misunderstanding of human sexuality, whose tragic sequelae we identify as the unhealed wound.

Misreading this metaphor is no small distortion; indeed, so committed is the official Church to a literal understanding of virgin birth that, emotionally and institutionally, it is extremely difficult, if not impossible, for the structure to achieve the perspective from which to view its deeper and broader spiritual meaning. As we can sense the almost muscular asceticism by which John Paul II has compelled himself to observe the abstract celibate ideal, we can also appreciate how he has dug deep the foundation of his own life on the literal meaning of virginity. At the center of his prayer life and of his political overtures stands the Virgin Mary. The Black Madonna of Czestochowa is, according to one biographer, "the most venerated virgin in the world as the defender of Poland and symbol of the Catholic faith," to whom he paid "homage as soon as he came home on his first papal visit."[9]

The biographer also describes the death of John Paul II's mother in 1929, just before the future pope turned nine. "The presence of death would never leave the consciousness of Karol Wojtyla. . . . His cult of Mary flowered from his mother's death: the natural identification."[10] One does not criticize or trifle with any man's inner life, especially not a man as great as John Paul II, but one can conclude that so profoundly personal is his understanding of the Virgin—he credits the Virgin of Fátima with saving his life after he was shot in 1981—and her role in working out his destiny that it strongly influences his total investment in the myth of Mary's virginity as a literal physical reality and so the basis for a reading of virginity as, by divine fiat, the highest and purest human state.

THE SPIRITUAL MEANING OF THE VIRGIN BIRTH

The metaphor of Virgin Birth is found throughout history, often applied, as Joseph Campbell notes, to "heroic personages or legendary figures who have given themselves totally to great causes."[11] The Virgin Birth refers, in this historical context, to a spiritual insight rather than a biological condition. It refers to that state "when in the mind and heart the ideal is conceived of a life lived, not for the primary economic and biological ends of survival, progeny, prosperity, and a little fun, but to a metaphysical end, intending values transcendent of historical survival."[12] Everyone is, therefore, capable of such a Virgin Birth, a coming to life through a new vision of the transcendent nature of reality. That is the rich, almost inexhaustible connotation of a metaphor that, if shrunken to its denotation, refers to a much more limited biological state valued hierarchically as one placed by God above all other conditions of existence.

Virgin Birth is a metaphor of wonder that is found almost everywhere—from American Indian lore to Greek mythology, in which many heroes are described as begotten of Zeus. It is suggested, in the Old Testament Book of Judges, chapter 13, that Samson was so born as well. The drastic shriveling of this metaphor of religious mystery to a narrow, concrete historical incident both dishonors religious language and destroys religious mystery. It may be understood, in our reading of a larger encompassing myth, as a result of that disastrous encounter in which the Grail King, seeking again that Grail as a literal goal even though it is actually a metaphor, slays the knight out of the East who symbolizes Nature, only to be himself gravely wounded sexually. So the Institution, for its own structural ends, has slain Nature through a forced transformation of the spiritual truth of the Virgin Birth into the concrete reality of a biological state. This has obscured the religious metaphor's real meaning and accentuated the division of flesh and spirit that causes this chronically painful and unhealed wound in humankind.

We are diminished and injured by the misreading of this metaphor, defended stoutly and aggressively by the official Church and fashioned into a pillar of celibate piety that hides the many sexual problems and unhappy adjustments that are the result of what can best be understood, as we have repeatedly noted, as an exercise of power by men over other men. The official Church has adopted many defenses that permit it to deny the sexual wounding taking place in the exaltation of and insistence on an abstraction of what, more often than not, ends as a psychic mutilation of human sexual functioning.

THE REVELATION OF DISORDER

Discussion of celibacy and chastity as the prime virtues demanded of the men and women who give themselves in service to the Institution has for a long time been impossible. Celibacy and chastity are treated, unknowingly, of course, by Church officials as fruit from the tree of the knowledge of Good and Evil at the center of their institutional Eden. One plucks and splits it open at the risk, not to the individual but to the Institution, of revealing how spotted and unhealthy are all but the margins of its tissues. Indeed, it yields the knowledge of Good and Evil so confounded with each other that the tree deserves to be withered, as the fig tree was by Jesus and for the same reason: a bad tree cannot bear good fruit.

If all the results of the enforced sexual innocence that have followed from the misunderstanding of Gospel sayings and the concrete misreading of the metaphors of religious mystery remain healthy, as the Institution and its leaders claim, then they hardly need to be kept from us. For of healthy things—of sunlight, fresh air, friendship, and love—we can never get enough. And of unhealthy things—of perverse or immature sexuality or of vice counterfeited into virtue to conceal gratification—we have already had too much. The outcome of centuries of dividing people into compartments of flesh and spirit instead of helping them to experience their wholeness and unity has made healthy people feel guilty for having healthy feelings and instincts. It has also made unhealthy people feel superior because of, rather than in spite of, their numbness to or alienation from healthy human sexual functioning.

That even great popes draw on inapplicable proof texts from scripture to bolster forgoing sexual relationships is melancholy evidence of how necessary the maintenance of the control of human sexuality remains for its present organization. So necessary has this discipline become to the Church as an Institution that, in Western countries, the bishops, their collegial spirit lost by their ready cooperation in their own emasculation, are willing to suffer enormous losses in order to keep celibacy in place among the clergy. Such leaders accept their own impotence, for example, in the operational suppression of their national conferences so that they accept—indeed, make themselves accessories to—the denial of the Eucharist to their Catholic people by refusing to allow married priests or women priests to celebrate this indispensable sacrament of identity and unity. What can it be about the rejection of marriage and the superiority of the so-called higher celibate life that can justify such an extraordinary abandonment of basic pastoral service to their people?

The defense of celibacy is unconvincing but tenacious. Only as the once intensely isolated Catholic culture opened itself, through the expanded educational opportunities ironically provided by the Institution and through the transactions of Vatican II, did the controls on celibacy begin to falter. You cannot allow sunshine into a once shuttered institution without stimulating what is healthy in those dwelling within. And you cannot let fresh air in without exposing the decay of centuries. In effect, that is what occurred as the Catholic community rejoined the human community. We discovered what was healthy, but we also learned of the unhealthy things that had thrived in the darkness.

THE GOOD, THE BAD, THE UNHEALTHY

Perhaps the least healthy response of the Institutional Church is found in its almost desperate unwillingness to examine how the celibate ideal is translated into the real-life experience of priests. If it did, it would have to release its deadman's grasp on the controls of human sexual expression. One need not have an advanced degree in psychology, however, to agree that if something is healthy, it can stand exposure to sunlight and fresh air. We signal at least our uncertainty about the healthiness of an activity or a belief if we hide it, as people do betraying love letters, or deny it, as people do pathological behavior.

The refusal to allow the world's bishops to discuss celibacy at Vatican II remains irrefutably unhealthy, as do the papal efforts, howsoever rationalized, to end any and all discussion at any level in the Church about celibacy or about even the possibility of ordaining women to the priesthood. No man can be named a bishop by Pope John Paul II unless his record is clear of any dissent, no matter how measured or mild, on these issues or on the third great sexually charged question, birth control.

There is no available protocol for discussing these matters with the present pope or of any of the Vatican congregations that set their agenda less as a response to the needs of the world than to the wishes of the Pope. Bureaucrats go to their offices every day to prevent rather than to facilitate reflection on questions that might send tremors through their structures. Therefore, it is difficult to find a proper forum in which, with all due respect, to disagree with the Pope without being branded anti-papal or disloyal. Yet disagree we must if what is healthy is put at risk by defenses whose transparency betrays their mottled and markedly unhealthy character.

The first question on such a hypothetical agenda would be, What do we really know about celibacy and sexuality in the life experience of priests?

AFTER BRICK AND MORTAR

One does not exaggerate by observing that the Brick and Mortar era did for American Catholicism exactly what these elements do for any structure: they bind it securely together, keep it safe from storms, allow a life in which one can hardly hear the traffic noise of the larger host culture. Once this era ended, literally and psychologically, such a gated community of Catholic life could no longer live unto itself and away from the rest of the world.

One result was the lowering of the once automatic defenses of clergy behavior so that the widespread underlying long-term problematic sexual adjustments of some priests could no longer be hidden or benignly ignored. One must sympathize with those many men who, having entered the seminary in high school, lived in a highly controlled but highly supportive Catholic environment until their ordination. Only after that moment of release—much like launching a ship so that the freedom to enter the seas' depths also makes it vulnerable to their hidden rocks and corrosive feast of rust—were they exposed to the real-world environment in which their previously hushed and protected problems of personal growth and sexual identity assailed and bewildered them.[13] The result was the rapid dissolution of such features of the Brick and Mortar culture as sustaining the sometimes immature camaraderie of rectory life and consequent changes in the lifestyles and living conditions of priests.

During this period of cultural transformation, many heterosexual priests sought from the official Church its dispensation from celibacy and permission to marry. While these men were often thought of, and branded, as weak in virtue and as failures to the Institution, indeed, as deserters, subsequent developments suggest that as a group they were responding to their healthy instincts. The Institution could not contain them—that is, accommodate what was fundamentally sound and human in their seeking relationships of intimacy—because it could not, and would not, make room for them within cells and sanctuaries built only for men. A generation and more has passed, and the stability of former priests in their marriages, family life, and success in real-world occupations makes it difficult to sustain their earlier dismissal as less dedicated than the priests who remained behind. It may be concluded that a substantial core of healthy men departed from the priesthood, altering the proportion of the mature to the immature among those who remained.[14]

LIVE MEN DYING

A decade later the clerical scandal of pedophilia exploded as towering bins of grain do, not from outer attack but from within, out of the dangerous mist of dust that rises from the packed-down and airless conditions in the dark. Then we were greeted with the tragic revelations of the miserable, furtive, and immature personality growth of many priests, of which their preying, helplessly, on young boys, helpless, was a major symptom. The institutionally repressed priesthood revealed the price men had paid to allow the Institution to maintain absolute control over a celibate condition whose undeveloped inner reality it had left unexamined, despite the data from the extensive 1971 study of the American priesthood that indicated the varied states, some of them highly marginal, of personal development among the clergy.[15]

These costs include the harm visited on thousands of trusting children by the supposedly trustworthy clergy. Encompassed as well is the suffering of the offending priests themselves—few, if any, of whom consciously chose the priesthood in order to have access to or exploit boys and girls. So, too, their families grieve, especially their mothers, who in the Brick and Mortar phase were thought specially chosen by the applauding culture. They had once gloried in watching the solemn ordination ceremonies of their sons, whose fingers were bound in the ritual linen bands that would bind their own in death. Now they wept as their sons, their once consecrated hands now manacled, were taken from courtrooms to prisons, sometimes virtually abandoned by the official Church.

Because the older self-contained culture, despite its brick and mortar, had largely collapsed, the discreet protection and management of sexually conflicted priests could no longer be sustained. They were once sent for treatment, often to centers far from their home dioceses, and after their release somewhat routinely reassigned to other parishes, where they sometimes abused children again. After his conviction and imprisonment as a result of his homosexual activity, Oscar Wilde was once left, in his prison uniform, standing on a station platform as a trainload of commuters gazed on his public shame. In effect, this is what has happened to dozens of once culturally shielded priests: they have been left under the shaming gaze of the entire culture, their crimes manifest, their once high calling brought miserably low. Their sexual wounds and their sexual wounding were revealed as the castle bridge was raised behind them, Knights of the Grail no more.

For the first time, the voices of the abused were given a hearing. The wound had always been closed without healing in Brick and Mortar times, when the offending priest was given a cover story and transferred, and those abused had been told never again to speak of their having been violated. As the painful truth poured out, all could glimpse the weeping wound of officially controlled sexuality in the lives of both the abusers and the abused. In a review of studies of sexual abuse, the sequelae include "increased rates of post-traumatic stress disorder, major depression, anxiety disorders, borderline personality disorder, paranoia dissociation, somaticization, bulimia, anger, aggressive behavior, poor self-image, poor school performance, running away from home and legal trouble."[16]

Once the veil had been torn away from this long, secret suffering, monetary costs rose steeply from the insurance claims and the civil suits, once culturally unthinkable, lodged against clerical offenders, their bishops, and their dioceses. The sheer number of these incidents exacted from the Institution another price that it found itself unwilling or unable to pay—a disinterested official effort to frame and answer the questions about the genesis of this unhealthy epidemic. This latter obligation, in a scandal that comes near to matching that of pedophilia itself, has not been honored, much less paid. It has rather been ignored by official responses that have sought to contain rather than to understand a problem that streams like blood from the larger unhealed sexual wound in the official Church.

Striking to this day is the manner in which the official Church has dealt with this problem that, at the very least, suggests that the attraction and living experience of the celibate life is more complex than it had at one time seemed. Rather than examine the issue directly, however, as any Church with a claim to judge the morality of others might be expected to do, its bishops have reacted with institutional reflexes to manage and control rather than with their pastoral gifts to understand and heal.

Largely following the advice of lawyers and insurers, they have responded much as the executives of United Carbide did after poisonous gas leaked from its Bophal, India, plant and settled as a cloud of death on hundreds of local people. The company's immediate and primary goal was to protect institutional assets, to admit nothing, to take a hard line in litigation, to settle legal actions reluctantly if at all, and to handle every occurrence on a case-by-case basis. The Church's decision about pedophilia, whose pastoral character is hard if not impossible to discern, is still operative and explains why, despite the obvious need, its bishops have developed no national policy to identify and deal with accusations of sexual impropriety by the clergy. This position was exemplified in an extraordinarily hard and clear fashion by Bishop Edward Egan of Bridgeport, Connecticut, who was named archbishop of New York in April 2000. A canon lawyer by training, he designated priests charged with sexual crimes as "independent contractors"—the diocese had no legal obligations for their actions—thus cutting himself and the diocese free from even curiosity about its priests' behavior or problems.

Archbishop Egan did not become the Pope's personal choice for this high-profile position by advocating such policies in an institutional vacuum. Can we conclude other than that he has the Pope's approval for stonewalling on sexual abuse charges against the clergy, for practicing the equivalent of priest abandonment to protect institutional assets, and for planning vigorous countersuits against anybody's claiming to have been sexually abused by priests? Such a development is nothing short of public scandal on the part of the Institution. It reveals, tragically, that this Institution is more comfortable keeping its sexual wound unhealed than in healing it. That is an empty triumph of illness over health.

In February 1986 Joseph Cardinal Bernardin, then archbishop of Chicago and one of the most influential leaders in postconciliar American Catholicism, asked me and my wife, a psychiatrist who had extensive experience in working with priests, to draw up a proposal that would take an exceedingly modest first step, a review of the literature, on pedophilia and associated developmental sexual problems of priests. He submitted it to the National Conference of Catholic Bishops through its then secretary, Monsignor Daniel Hoye, to seek its approval and to proceed with the work. A few weeks later Monsignor Hoye wrote to say that he had referred the suggestion to the committee that dealt with clergy issues and that, in conference with them, it was concluded that the body of bishops would not take any positive action.

The proposal was not submitted then, nor a few years later when Cardinal Bernardin was pushing for a national policy on sexual abuse by the clergy and other Church personnel. After that initiative was also rebuffed by the body of bishops, the cardinal moved to develop guidelines for the archdiocese of Chicago in such matters.[17] These guidelines were widely copied throughout the country, but as the millennium dawned, the bishops had still failed to adopt a national policy on this subject. The wound remains unhealed.[18]

DEFENDING AND PURSUING CELIBACY

✝

DESPITE THE BITTER HARVEST of sexual abuse among Catholic priests, celibacy remains off-limits to any serious study by or within the official Church. Its value has been reasserted by Pope John Paul II, who rejects any modification in this requirement as vigorously as he does any change in the all-male requirement of the priesthood, even though the scriptural and theological foundations for such positions are hardly secure.

The Pope is true to the vision of the Church on which he built his own remarkable life. If he tolerates no dissent, it may be because he has allowed no dissent within himself to this ideal. And while he has welcomed scientists of every kind to the Vatican and has even rehabilitated the once condemned Galileo, he has not permitted even the possibility of any scientific investigation of celibacy. This requirement, sometimes termed a discipline and at others a virtue, has consequently been so variously defended and defined as to deepen doubts about the healthiness of these often tortured interpretations. The celibate priest remains the protected person in John Paul II's Institutional Church, with an inner life as sacred and set off as a sanctuary.

However, a better understanding of the priest's psychosexual development and functioning would yield truths that, in the long run, no person need fear. In the same way, the styles of recruiting, evaluating, and educating a new generation of seminary candidates open a window on the dynamics of this overall process. Their personal maturity has already been a subject of so much discussion and opinion that it could only benefit from careful professional scrutiny. What is healthy, as we have noted, never fears sunlight and the open air.

IN GROANS INEXPRESSIBLE . . .

It may be helpful to review the simple definition of celibacy in the Code of Canon Law because it recapitulates the history, scriptural basis, and dimensions of the ideal: clerics "are *obliged to observe perfect and perpetual continence for the sake of the kingdom* and therefore are *obliged to observe celibacy,* which is *a special gift of God,* by which sacred ministers can adhere more easily to Christ with *an undivided heart and can more freely dedicate themselves to the service of God and humankind* [emphasis added]."[1]

On the first anniversary of Pope John Paul II's defense of priestly celibacy, then Archbishop, now Cardinal, J. Francis Stafford gave a talk at a Roman conference on the priesthood titled "Eucharistic Foundation of Sacerdotal Celibacy."[2] It is an extraordinary document in its ambition to demonstrate the spiritual incompatibility between priesthood's coexisting with marriage, notwithstanding the married state of the first pope.

Cardinal Stafford asserts that the "priest is celibate because he offers the one sacrifice in the person of the second Adam, whose unique sacrifice on the cross instituted his irrevocable covenantal union with the second Eve in one flesh of the new covenant." It is reasonable, he continues, "to postulate . . . a liturgical sacramental/symbolic incongruity between the exercise of priestly order and entering into the marriage bond. . . . *It is because of the priest's own nuptial integration into the sacrifice he offers that only a man is capable of acting in the person of the head and can be a priest. . . . He cannot marry without that betrayal of his own nuptiality, which is analogously adulterous; his exclusive dedication to the bride of Christ bars any secondary self-donation* [emphasis added]."

This frankly sexual argument is expressed in achingly abstract terms: the "commitment of personal nuptiality is inseparable from offering the one sacrifice. . . . It underlies the celibate nuptiality of *Pastores Dabo Vobis* [the Pope's 1992 letter on celibacy]. Whether it be to the wife in the consummation of the marriage or to the Church in the offering of the one sacrifice, the masculine nuptial self-donation is exclusive and permanent."

One may examine this document with respect, and yet many questions, for its author. It is filled with the "donation of self" language of John Paul II as it attempts to make of celibacy a profound condition for the priest's being a faithful husbandlike figure in a marriage to the bridelike Church, with his fulfilling his marital sexuality (nuptiality) in a purified state through his celebration of the Eucharist. Pure and single, Stafford asserts, are the conditions for taking on this celibate husband's sexual-like obligations to his bride, the Church. Thus, "for the priest, it is the sacramental one flesh of the new covenant. In both cases, the self-donation by the head is the offering of sacrifice, the payment of the debt. It is at the same time an election of the bride: It is for the exclusive benefit of the body."

This argument may not be persuasive to any reader with any experience with marriage—or, for that matter, with celibacy. It is, however, the institutional argument par excellence. This is a complex rationalization of celibacy offered by a high-placed and well-intentioned cleric to other high-placed clerics, employing the high-flown language calculated to please the highest of all high-placed clerics, the Pope himself, the source of this philosophical idealization of a condition that is as removed from sexual or celibate experience as cold clear stars are from life on earth. This is the Institution talking to itself, blinding itself to the unhealed wound, which only bleeds more profusely under the pressure of such strangely asexual sexual argumentation.

Above all, one feels the strenuous exertions that go into this line of reasoning, this man-made diversion of the waters, a great engineering feat to harness the energy of a two-hearted river in order to keep the lights on, the unions out, and all shifts working in an Institution operating on nineteenth-century time. This kind of argument is made not to invite questions but to assure its audience that there are no questions to be asked. In this case, the reassurance is supposed to arise from bolstering the defenses that once and for all, in the obsolete actuarial language applied to the marriage bed as the place to pay the marriage "debt," justify the intrinsically sacred and inviolable character of an all-male celibate priesthood from which, by these same uncomfortable theological assertions, women are forever barred. It is, in short, the divine plan and is, therefore, out of our hands.

This is asexuality in action, daring to reveal itself by drawing on the mystery of marriage as two in one flesh to justify the spiritualization of the never-ending wedding night of the priest with the "new Eve" of the Church. Instead of convincing readers, however, such argumentation makes them uneasy. Their kindest response is to turn away from this embarrassing, abstract pseudosexuality that has no relationship to or resonation within the human experience of love, marriage, or sexuality.

This is a shadow argument offered, one may allow, with goodwill but in an institutional formulation that attempts to rationalize and buttress an official position that is eroding badly from within. It is a surface argument that excuses while it forbids anybody from looking beneath this veneer, so fragile as to be scraped away with a fingernail, into the actual life experience of priests. This argument is asexual, as were the arguments for the castrati, boys rendered asexual through forced sacrifices of their sexual potency, exacted in the name of a polyphony in which one could hear the sweet but corrupted voice of the Institution that oversaw the practice with the indifference of a caliph to the mutilated guards of his harem.

Such asexuality is the ecclesiastical counterpart—or, better, the reverse image—of the secular sexual profligacy that such neutered clergy enthusiastically condemn. These are twins separated at birth, this brutal abstinence and brutalized eroticism that betray and proclaim immaturity, a lack of growth and integration of sexuality into human personality. What is it that ails you? The Church and the world answer with one voice—the unhealed wound of sexuality that leaves us with no place where, in comfort and peace, we can sit, stand, or lie down.

POWER OVER AUTHORITY:
THE ASEXUAL SYNDROME

If asexuality is violent in the energy with which it argues for and enforces arguments for a celestial celibate sexual state, what explains and what does this violence sound like as it manipulates assent to a divinized celibate condition? Even the most dispassionate cannot fail to identify the recurring common elements in the asexual style. Salient among these is the hardly subtle sexual gratification it delivers to those who justify their dominance of others as a right flowing from the inherent spiritual superiority of chastity, celibacy, and an all-male priesthood.

This may be better understood as an assertion of power rather than as an expression of authority. As discussed earlier, the goal of power, or unhealthy authoritarianism, is always control of the other. The goal of healthy authority (from *augere*, "to grow, to increase") is the full human development of the other. Pope John Paul II is a tragic figure because he is truly a great man whose vulnerability—heartbreaking for him, heartrending for Catholics—arises from his confounding of power and authority so that as he uses power to control the Church as an Institution, he spends down his true authority to help it grow as a People of God.

The often cheerless advocates of this falsely divinized, and therefore dehumanized, celibacy cannot suppress a certain tone of superiority, of celebrating themselves as true believers, as a faithful remnant defending the authentic ancient faith. They write off as neomodernists those scripture scholars and theologians who reveal the inappropriate and often irrelevant character of their own treasured proof texts about celibacy and chastity. This complacency—this certainty that they possess the truth—bears an unmistakable family resemblance to the untroubled confidence of the Roman Inquisition that it possessed knowledge about the universe superior to that of Galileo, whom they condemned in the sixteenth century. The Roman Inquisition, as noted, was headquartered in the present offices of the Congregation for the Doctrine of the Faith from which so many pronouncements, judgments, and punishments about human sexuality have been issued with similarly misplaced confidence in recent years.

BUREAUCRATIC GRATIFICATIONS

The asexual style is marked by a rejection of dialogue, despite its surface invitation to theologians to enter a conversation about aspects of their writings with which their investigators find fault. It must be remembered, of course, that this congregation, headed by Joseph Cardinal Ratzinger, is essentially a bureaucracy whose existence depends on finding fault and flaws rather than in giving praise or encouragement to others.

If, for those under investigation, virtue must be its own reward, bureaucracy is its own gratification for the investigators. Bureaucracies, as noted, are not interested in solving but in protracting problems. Their ongoing existence depends on keeping the problem, and thereby themselves, alive. The bureaucratic response of the Church as an Institution is therefore directly opposed to the pastoral response of the Church as a People. The latter raises a sacramental sign of healing that understands and eases the wounds of intimacy so they may mend, as all healthy things do, from within so that the injured may emerge stronger at the broken places. The

Brick and Mortar bureaucracy raises a sign of contradiction that is gratified by probing the wounds of intimacy, keeping them open to extend its own obsessive, voyeuristic, and often perverse gratification.

THE CODE NAPOLEON IN THE CITY OF GOD

The Code Napoleon lives again in such bureaucratic procedures, for *the accused are expected to prove their innocence* for crimes of which they are presumed guilty. This is power grotesquely masquerading as authority, degrading its claims to the latter as it systematically degrades those it questions. It is here, perhaps, that these officials, at least half in love with the rustle of the silken garments of ecclesiastical office, pay this misconstrued "marriage debt" to the Church, replenishing their power as they gratify their need to exercise it over others. That is the sexual transaction at the core of the "use of power by men over other men."

The asexual style clothes itself in superfluous secrecy, binding those whom it investigates to silence about the nature and content of the procedures and hearings into which they may be drawn to "explain" their writings, teachings, or even, as in recent cases of work with homosexuals, their pastoral ministry. If such secrecy does not seem compatible for the Church of Jesus, who spoke of doing things always "in the light," it does match the bureaucratic institutional needs of the official Church.

Such a mentality arises not from Christ or the early Church but from "as early as the sixth and seventh centuries," as theologian Franz Josef Von Beeck writes, when "bishops and abbots were becoming part of the emergent *administrative* structure of the West; in due course, they became 'peers'—peers, that is, of the barons and counts and viscounts and dukes and kings, just as the pope came to be regarded as the peer of the emperor. . . . Small wonder that the sacrament of orders became widely as well as dangerously associated with masculinity understood as power. . . . It is fair to suggest that preoccupation with power and jurisdiction has bedeviled the ordained ministry to this day."[3]

HUMILIATING THE HUMBLED

Abasement of the other, while defending against the correlated abasement of the self, is a major component of many unhealthy sexual transactions. This is often the invisible agenda item when an inquisitor denigrates the subject of inquiry by the defiling process of inquiry itself. The rubber hose alleged to be used in police questioning would be gentle and up front compared with the rituals of humiliation employed by self-satisfied Church officials in their dealings with men and women they suspect of heresy or disobedience.

As one who has had personal experience of being interrogated at the Congregation for the Doctrine of the Faith, I can empathize with all those healthy men and women who present themselves humbly in its offices to be humiliated in return. My case, only one and perhaps the least among thousands, concerned my petition to be dispensed from the obligation of celibacy and to leave the priesthood, or "return to the lay state," as canon law puts it, in order to marry.

Let us turn for a moment to the bureaucratic procedures to which such petitioners were subject in the 1970s. As Barbara Susan Balboni summarizes it:

> More telling is the Church's legal stance toward priests seeking laicization, that is, return to the lay state. Canon 280 states: "After it has been validly received, sacred ordination never becomes invalid." A priest can lose his clerical state (c.290), but if the priest seeks to resign after ordination, he has to agree that from the beginning his ordination was invalid. In other words, as far as

ordaining a priest is concerned, the Church cannot
make a mistake. . . . *To be laicized, the priest has to
declare as invalid all the years of his ministry* [italics
added]."[4]

Priests who sought laicization during the post–Vatican II period
were routinely advised by benign bureaucrats, but bureaucrats
nonetheless, to go along, in effect, with this presumption by testify-
ing (a) that they had never wanted to be priests in the first place or
(b) that they suffered from major psychiatric disabilities that made
them incapable of ever accepting ordination validly. This was a
seductive invitation: we will give you a discharge, dishonorable to
be sure but a discharge nonetheless, on the condition that you fal-
sify your life and work in order to fit into our statistical model of the
departing as self-admittedly mad or self-deluded about a calling
that never existed.

MY CASE, AMONG MANY

It is not surprising that many American priests refused to degrade
themselves by lying about their lives in order to win the approval of
the Vatican bureaucracy. While Pope Paul VI at least allowed this
process to continue for priests seeking honorable exits from the clerical life, Pope John Paul II for many years refused to allow any permissions to be granted, unilaterally suspending Church law that allowed
them. This added a new note of humiliation for men who, wishing to
be honest about themselves, were now told not only that the truth
was not acceptable but that their asking for permission to marry,
even though provided for in canon law, was also unacceptable. This
was also humiliating for the women they intended to marry, as they
were characterized, if their existence was even noted, as partners and
accessories in relationships that many officials refused to acknowledge as anything but failures of both faith and flesh.

Except for Pope Paul VI's single line about love as conquering sorrow in priests' marriages, bureaucrats have avoided, as they would a threatening rock in a safe asexual harbor, the intrinsically heterosexual dynamic of marriage. To this day in this process, the woman, as individual and symbol, remains a non-person, ruled out of the range of perception as the black players were by Jimmy Breslin's cops as they watched basketball.[5]

A prime reason given for refusing permissions for more than a dozen years was that it would be "scandalous" to allow former priests to take their places in the Catholic community. As only one of a multitude, I was informed that if I wanted permission to marry, I would have to abandon my university professorship and move out of Chicago. Nor was I allowed to give a public lecture within the archdiocese of Chicago. These were punitive aspects of an immense fiction that the official Church endorsed about the low and unacceptable character of those men who attempted to withdraw honorably from the priesthood. In my case, the Roman congregation that was once the Holy Office also humiliated such church leaders as Chicago's Joseph Cardinal Bernardin and New York's John Cardinal O'Connor by turning down their endorsement of my petition. My permission came through only after I was forced by illness to give up regular teaching and was judged no longer to be giving "public scandal."

REDUCTION BY RESCRIPT

Few former priests think that this bureaucratic intention to debase them represents the healthier part of the Church as a People or the voice of Jesus himself, and many knew or were referred to priests who used their pastoral judgment to celebrate their marriages. As couples, they went on to locate in parishes whose members, having more significant things to worry about, were not scandalized by their becoming part of their communities. When rescripts of laicization finally arrive, their language and tone express the asexual punitiveness that is advertised as the "reduction" of a man to the "lay state," a diminishing process for the hierarchical imagination and a testament to a divided view of the human person in which the passage from "higher" to "lower" renders him down to a condition of "otherness" or "depersonalization," the final distillation of the great vats and machines in which totalitarian states process dissidents.

In this instrument of laicization one feels less a pastoral permission than a military dismissal in which, as in the ancient ceremony of defrocking the cleric in the chapel or the military ritual of dishonorably discharging the officer on the parade ground, the person must be stripped of his rank and identifying symbols, denuded, as Adam and Eve were, to be cloaked more in shame than in fig leaves, on being expelled from the ecclesiastical Eden.

The document is also a hospital chart of the unhealed wound in institutional Catholicism, for in its reluctant permission to marry, one is struck that the bride is not invited to the wedding, that institutional reflexes keep her outside the procedure and ignore marriage as a sacramental relationship between a man and a woman. No, the man alone is dealt with, the better to complete his emasculation. Thus, in the current draft, issued now by the Congregation of Divine Worship and the Discipline of the Sacraments, the rescript reads, in part:

> This rescript takes effect from the moment of its notification. . . . It includes inseparably the dispensation from priestly celibacy as well as the loss of the clerical state. It is never lawful for the petitioner to disjoin these two elements, i.e., to accept the first and to refuse the second. . . . With regards to the celebration of a canonical marriage, the . . . ordinary should see to it that such arrangements are carried out with caution and without pomp or outward display. . . . The ecclesiastical author-

ity . . . should exhort him to participate in the life of the people of God in a manner which is in harmony with his new condition of life. . . . But at the same time he should inform him of the following: (a) A dispensed priest . . . loses the rights proper to the clerical state and his ecclesiastical dignities and offices. . . . (b) He remains excluded from the exercise of the sacred ministry. . . . He cannot, therefore, give a homily. . . . He cannot discharge the extraordinary ministry of distributing Holy Communion nor can he perform a directive office in the pastoral field. (c) He . . . cannot perform any functions in seminaries or equivalent institutions. In other institutions of higher studies which depend in any manner whatsoever upon ecclesiastical authority, he cannot discharge a directive function or the office of teaching. (d) In institutions which do not depend upon ecclesiastical authority, he cannot teach any discipline that is properly theological or closely connected with it. (e) In institutions of lesser studies which depend upon ecclesiastical authority, he cannot discharge any directive office or the office of teaching unless the ordinary, according to his prudent judgment and with scandal removed, should judge to decide otherwise with regard to the role of teaching. . . . Per se, a priest dispensed from priestly celibacy and a fortiori a priest who is married must not live in places where his previous condition is known. . . . Lastly, some work of piety or charity should be imposed on the petitioner. . . . A brief report should be sent to this Congregation concerning the execution of the rescript, and if there is any wonderment on the part of the faithful, a prudent explanation should be provided. All other contrary provisions not withstanding . . .

As a distinguished former priest observed when he received his rescript, "Catholic convicts on death row have more rights in the

Church than I do." As former priests have, as a group, constituted no threat to the Church in their subsequent lives, the institution's need to protect itself from them and the harsh conditions it metes out to them suggest that heterosexual relationships remain mysteriously and pervasively threatening to the asexual bureaucracy.

A NEW BALANCE

Nonetheless, these official transactions—this exercise of power by men over other men—have continued with undeniable self-righteousness even as the *Titanic* of the official Church slit itself open on the long-submerged ice dagger of priest pedophilia. This tragic development, with its full measure of pain for priest-pedophiles, their families, and their victims, has cracked but not broken the shield of the bureaucratic asexual style. Nor, as noted, have officials evinced much interest in diagnosing the roots of this problem.

This willful ignorance about causation is to them more bearable than the earthy truth because the problem can be invested with the illusion of control by being isolated, denied, and, in effect, secularized for management by lawyers and insurers, so that, as noted, the most visible of American Church officials, Archbishop Edward Egan of New York, could claim, in his previous diocese of Bridgeport, Connecticut, that the official Church had no responsibility for priests accused of pedophilia. Priests, he continues to claim, are "independent contractors," freelance ministers rather than, as they are regarded in every other aspect of their lives, attached to and dependent on the Institution for their identity and livelihood.

Denial is the least healthy of all psychological defenses, and it is no less so in this abandonment of priests by the bishop to whom, on their ordination day, they must promise obedience. This denial of relationship to the official Church ignores canon law but does insulate the official Church and its assets from any claims made against pedophile priests in civil cases. We may be dismayed but hardly surprised to read in *The New York Times* that "when he is asked about accusations of pedophilia by clergy members in Bridge-port, he . . . responds with a terse 'No comment,' to avoid supplying any usable television sound bites. . . . In 1993, the Bridgeport dio-cese was sued by 31 plaintiffs, claiming abuse by 8 priests over more than 30 years. Under Bishop Egan, the diocese's lawyers have aggressively fought the complaints, and he has been criticized for refusing to discuss accusations and for making no overtures to the plaintiffs."[6]

Archbishop, at this writing, perhaps cardinal at your reading, Edward Egan was not appointed to such a prestigious assignment unless Vatican officials, and presumably the Pope himself, knew of and thereby tacitly approved of this classically asexual and amoral mode of responding to pedophilia in the priesthood. Thus, denial and dissociation are validated as hardball tactics by the Institution itself, that seems content, as self-serving organizations always are, to sacrifice a certain number of lives to save itself. Here we may encounter the truly last and greatest of treasons, to do the wrong thing for what is always blessed as the right reason, "the good of the Church," that mocks itself in the denied erotic reward of binding priests and yet abandoning them as well.

The exit of priests to marry—and the very idea of a man and a woman in love—remains imaginatively inadmissable and essen-tially dishonorable because it cannot be denied and cannot be con-trolled by ecclesiastics. In this transparent sexual dynamic, heterosexual love and marriage are threatening to the asexual bureaucrat because his gratification depends on the other's cooper-ation in the a priori degradation of his marriage and submission by him, and by the woman he wishes to marry, to the shaming condi-tions of the rescript. To this mean universe we may apply to those oppressed sexually by the Institution, the lines Chesterton wrote to his hospitalized wife, "You will burn up this world at last, you are too healthy for the world."

The National Conference of Catholic Bishops in the United States has resisted any effort to understand the pedophilia crisis or the myriad associated concerns about the level of psychosexual maturity among candidates for the priesthood. The bishops, as a group, have not been able to overcome the institutional dynamics that they are pressed by Rome to honor even if they disagree with them. Their response is not spontaneous and healthy but calculated and officious, the same kind of denial employed by large corporations, such as tobacco companies when faced with the evidence that their product is a cause of cancer. Church officials, with few exceptions, have resolutely refused to consider that the complex sociopsychological factors in the celibate clerical culture may contribute to the problem of pedophilia or to other problematic conditions, including the homosexualization of the priesthood.

DEMASCULINIZING THE PRIESTHOOD

As we have observed, it is a knight's journey and more from Spencer Tracy's unquestionably masculine Father Flanagan in 1938's *Boys Town* to the fey and self-centered priest of 1999's *The Sopranos*. The popular arts track and reflect human experience, and who can be surprised at such an outcome after decades of institutional emasculation of priests? For just as the full-blooded woman has been made invisible to institutional eyes in the process of "reducing a cleric to the lay state," so now the full-blooded, confident male has been reduced to the diffusely identified and uncertain figure in the American priesthood. What is it that ails the Grail King, we may ask sympathetically, that he should feel his genital wound so keenly that he is so uneasy, so beyond comfort? Is this the lesion he sustained in that very moment when he slew Nature in the name of the Spirit? Why, we must ask, should we be surprised that the priesthood has lost its virile character and its potency?

Some observers speculate that the priests who sought laiciza-tion, instead of being, as they were characterized, traitors to the chaste life, constituted, in fact, a healthy heterosexual cohort who withdrew from an unhealthy environment. "Their absence," according to Father Donald Cozzens, ". . . has dramatically changed the gay/straight ratio and contributed to the disproportionate num-ber of priests with homosexual orientation [and] . . . has created a gay subculture in most of the larger U.S. dioceses . . . and in many of our seminaries."[7]

This experienced seminary rector and vicar for priests sees the change in the composition of Church culture as problematic for laypeople and for straight priests and seminarians. The latter feel "out of sync"; as a heterosexual would feel if he wandered into a gay bar, "he just doesn't seem to fit in with the others [and] may suggest to the seminarian that he is not called to the priesthood."[8]

The plight also affects gays, for they "are likely to feel at home and at ease in a seminary with a significant gay population . . . because they instinctively recognize other gay seminarians, circles of support and camaraderie are quickly formed. . . . Not infre-quently, however, the sexual contacts and romantic unions among gay seminarians creates intense and complicated webs of intrigue and jealousy leading to considerable inner conflict. Here the sexu-ally ambiguous seminarian drawn into the gay subculture is particu-larly at risk."[9] The graduates of such a seminary may find themselves ill-prepared to minister to a parish culture in which homosexuality plays a smaller role and in which their conflicted attitudes toward heterosexuality may cause them unanticipated problems.

THE JOHN PAUL II GENERATION

It is striking, for example, to note how many contemporary semi-narians, to whom all believers can wish only good, perceive them-selves in ways that set them at odds with the very people they are called to serve. They often see themselves as "new men" or "the John Paul II generation,"[10] saviors who will repair the damage they believe Vatican II caused the Church.

That at least some members of this self-styled elite are already practiced in the asexual style of shaming and humiliating others may be inferred from their description in a recent comprehensive study of Catholic theological seminaries: "The greatest challenge for faculty," is found in "those [students] who have a rigid understanding of their faith. . . . They create a climate of distrust and defensiveness, publicly questioning the orthodoxy of professors and fellow students."[11]

Indeed, this generation of seminarians seems to recapitulate many of the dynamics of a previous era—for example, in the restoration of and reverence given to the mother of the aspirant priest. Time seems to have stopped in one seminarian's home, which "thrummed with the quiet, vehement faith of his mother. . . . Hefty painted statuettes of Christ and the Virgin Mary stood before a window in the kitchen, and, in the living room . . . there was a small table covered with lace, where holy water, candles and a relic—a bone of St. Elizabeth Seton, the first American saint—were on display. 'I always prayed that the Lord would take my sons to be His holy priests . . . You know it's nothing you deserve. It's God's gift.' "[12]

It is not surprising then to find that the seminarians reproduce the pre–Vatican II focus on sexual sin. One seminarian complains that "lots of magazine covers don't reach Christian modesty. . . . There are half-naked women all over the place."[13] We are told that "during the White House sex scandal . . . seminarians had to grapple with the Starr report. Many did not; some who did went to confession for it afterward."[14] Another seminarian objected to the "contracepting" on the sitcom *Seinfeld* and stopped watching "but kept track of what was happening on the show to the very end from nonseminary friends."[15]

The freeze frame continues in the description of the class in which the seminarians are learning to prepare betrothed couples for marriage. The subject of teacher Sister Paula Jean Miller is "the theology of sexuality. . . . Drawing on Pope John Paul II's theology of the body, Miller explained that the 'total self-donation,' or 'self-gift,' is the goal for human relationships. . . . Contraception is a holding back of some very critical aspect of who I am. It's saying to you, I want you but I don't want your fertility."[16] The author notes that "a majority of Catholic theologians disagree with this position."[17]

These seminarians are eager to preach on birth control, a subject not "received" and so, in itself lacking in the validation bestowed by that special gift of believers, is seldom referred to by American pastors today. This new generation of seminarians, however, appears convinced that a restoration of old-fashioned Brick and Mortar moralizing is just what the world needs. One seminarian produces a tape of a lecture he gave to teenagers. He seems very pleased that he says what he feels nobody else does anymore, "that masturbation is always a seriously disordered act. . . . In itself it is always wrong."[18] If they are criticized, these seminarians—many of whom compile "thanks be to God" folders of compliments given to them for self-consolation—feel that Jesus was criticized for the same reasons. Perhaps it is more than appropriate that one of these seminarians should describe their plight of taking on the sinful world in terms of a Sylvester Stallone movie: "They have to climb up the cliff with no ropes, going backward. That is our life."[19]

These seminarians, perhaps much to their own later pain, have been well initiated into the asexual mode that so binds them that it may never occur to them that healing flows from the simple, non-judgmental question Parzival put to the sexually wounded Grail King, "What is it that ails you?" They are already convinced that all that is lacking is a reapplication of the divided image of human personality, and they do not seem aware of how gratified they are or how much their sense of potency depends on continuing to exacerbate humanity's sexual wound.

THE PENALTY PHASE

It is remarkable to note the style of discipline, as well as the penalties themselves, meted out by the official Church to those theologians and pastoral ministers who offer opinions about or try to ease the unhealed wound of human sexuality. In July 1999, for example, the Vatican ended the New Ways Ministry to Catholic homosexuals that had been instituted by Sister Jeannine Gramick and Father Robert Nugent in 1977. "Cardinal James Hickey of Washington [D.C.] . . . expressed opposition to their work for nearly 20 years—the approximate length of the Vatican investigation that led to last year's ban and silencing."[20]

The fierce self-confidence of the judges is obvious in the original condemnation: "The Congregation for the Doctrine of the Faith is obliged to declare that the positions advanced by Sister Jeannine Gramick and Father Robert Nugent regarding the *intrinsic evil of homosexual acts and the objective disorder of the homosexual inclination* are doctrinally unacceptable because they do not faithfully convey the clear and constant teaching of the Catholic Church in this area [emphasis added]."[21]

Described as an "expansion" of the 1999 directive, the co-workers were called to Rome as if to Canossa and were told that they were prohibited from speaking or writing about the ban or the ecclesiastical processes that led up to it, speaking or writing on matters related to homosexuality, protesting against the ban or encouraging the faithful to publicly express dissent from the official Magisterium (Church teaching authority), and criticizing the Magisterium in any public forum whatsoever concerning homosexuality or related issues. While Father Nugent accepted the directive to maintain his status as a priest, Sister Gramick refused, saying, "I choose not to collaborate in my own oppression by restricting a basic human right."[22]

What is astounding is the completeness of this penalty, which emasculated her priest colleague and is unmistakably aimed at eliminating Sister Gramick's human potency, her ability to create in any way or even to comment—requiring that she should, in effect, act as if bound by social pressure out of the Raj's India and immolate herself and her ministry. This extraordinary thoroughness, so that not a stone might be left upon a stone of her work, is a measure of the unconscious hostility of the officials who so sentenced her and of the asexual gratification they experienced by carrying it out.

This transaction, with its barely disguised sexual dynamics and defenses, was echoed by some American bishops who were eager to have their raised hands counted by their Roman superiors. Thus, Bishop Fabian Bruskewitz of Lincoln, Nebraska, wrote Sister Gramick a letter in which he said, "I have the right to formally prohibit you from speaking in this diocese. . . . This is hereby done by this letter."[23] The dynamics of this effort to exercise authority even over a site outside his jurisdiction are revealed in their astonishing primitivity in an editorial in the *Southern Nebraska Register*: "In a failed attempt to infect decent people with their ideological pathologies, the anti-Catholic sect Call to Action has recently reached into a theological sewer and brought Sister Jeanie Gramick SSND, an apostle of sexual perversion."[24]

THE BLOOD BE UPON YOU AND YOUR PARENTS

This asexually gratifying approach testifies to the wound of which it is a symptom. One need hardly be a trained psychiatrist to detect the discomfort with women, roaring beneath the ground like a coal mine fire, so that we can read its primitive force indirectly, in a signature of jagged cracks on the land. We encounter this rumbling dynamic in low-level unhealthy defenses that so blind their authors that they cannot recognize or properly name their own impulses. The dangerous fragility of such a manifestation can be observed in another recent punishment whose vindictiveness and completeness smacks of the revenge, deferred to other generations, in the Greek feuds described by novelist Harry Mark Petrakis.

Anne and Ed Reynolds had been members of the St. Aedan's Parish in Pearl River, New York, from its founding in 1966. Both were Eucharistic ministers, the husband since 1977, the wife since 1980. Parents of eight children, including a twenty-eight-year-old gay son, Andrew, they wrote a letter protesting the Vatican ban on Gramick and Nugent to the *Journal News* of Rockland County. In it they termed the Vatican language about gays "particularly distressing to parents. It is not pleasant to hear your loving and beloved child described as 'objectively disordered.' Neither is it pleasant to be told that a child's loving relationship with a longtime and faithful partner is 'intrinsically evil.'"

Noting that such language could incite prejudice and possibly violence toward homosexuals, they wrote that "as parents of a gay man, we cannot fully assent to the church's teaching on homosexuality. To do so would be to deny our son and violate our consciences." Their pastor, Monsignor Joseph Penna, was away when the letter was printed, on August 2, 1999, in the *Journal News* and on August 12 in the archdiocesan paper, *Catholic New York*. After he returned, he claimed that he had received complaints about its appearance and on Saturday, August 28, telephoned the Reynoldses to ask them to refrain from fulfilling their Sunday assignments as Eucharistic ministers, proposing a meeting with them the following Tuesday. Face-to-face, he explained the complaints about the contents of their letter. He quickly accepted Mr. Reynolds's offer to resign from that ministry.[25]

This story caused hardly a ripple at the time and has long since been washed away by the news torrents. Ed and Anne Reynolds, who see themselves as conservative Catholics, have, however, been given the same bath of shame and humiliation that the Institution employs to punish and to re-establish control over all people who question the official descriptions and condemnations of homosexuals because they do not match their own experience.

Yet, after this small, mean victory over two good people—a repetition of what has happened beyond any counting of it in the official Church—for their naming their own experience, their own parish pastor, perhaps going against his own heart, became nonetheless a willing collaborator in shaming them. Can we suppose that a mother and father who objected to the Vatican language of *disorder* and *evil* really deserved this violence so precisely targeted against them? This couple accepted the stinging rebuke to their healthiness of spirit, but they are not confused about what happened to them in the brutal transaction that took place suddenly last summer. They understand the humiliation that they reject. "We're both just tired of secrecy and shame," they said, letting their own intuitive health triumph over the unhealthiness of the Institution's best efforts at abasement. "We don't think we have anything to be shamed about."

"IN A BURNING WINDING SHEET HE LIES,
AND HIS GRAVE HAS GOT NO NAME . . ."
—OSCAR WILDE

The millennial year—named a jubilee year by Pope John Paul II and dedicated to forgiveness by, and begging forgiveness for, the Catholic Church—began with a *Kansas City Star* series on the number of priests suffering and dying from AIDS and a series of rejoinders from the official Church denying the gravity of the problem and accusing the paper and other researchers of using skewed statistics in such studies. To his great credit and perhaps the endangerment of his career, the local bishop, Raymond J. Boland, said of the deaths, among them that of the former priest president of Rockhurst College in Kansas City, "Much as we would regret it, it shows that human nature is human nature."

"Church leaders," it continued, "in the United States and at the Vatican declined requests to discuss the findings and the Vatican referred questions to local bishops."[26]

If we are not surprised to find the Institution using the legally prescribed tactics so common in secular enterprises, we cannot be surprised or falsely scandalized to learn that a certain number of priests are HIV-infected and that many have died of AIDS. A. W. Richard Sipe, who has monitored such cases in the United States, estimates that approximately seven hundred priests have died of this illness.[27] Statistics are difficult to obtain, however, even from an actuarial review of death certificates.

At this point, and irrespective of the illness that merely reflects the unhealed wound in the Church regarding human sexuality, one uncomfortably observes how readily officials manage the life cycle of priests so that they can deny—almost from the cradle of their ordination to their resting place after their requiem—that priests have sexual problems. It is at this point that the manipulation and deceit converge to force one to entertain the last and most bitter of hypotheses, that the official Church is corrupt and corrupting.

We have observed how the official Church treats priests seeking dispensations to marry punitively even when granting their requests. It also collects statistics in a way so shameful that it loses the freedom ever to criticize such papers as the *Kansas City Star* for the manner in which it researched the problem of AIDS among priests. We have seen how the official Church was able to use denial about priests seeking laicization by forcing them (a) to deny that they ever had a calling or (b) to affirm that their minds were clouded by serious mental illness, so that they could claim that *no* true priest had ever sought to leave the priesthood.

That spectacular dishonesty suborning dishonesty from good men can be understood as nothing other than corrupt in its rejection of truth and its knowing compilation of falsehood. It also avoids any examination of human sexual realities, thus raising a tattered shield to conceal against facing the unhealed wound in institutional Catholicism. The profound corruption of manipulating men's lives is trumped by the surpassing deceit of falsifying their deaths and, in many cases, even their identities. This is emasculation into the grave.

The Associated Press reports, for example, on "Bishop Emerson J. Moore, who left the Archdiocese of New York in 1995 and went to Minnesota, where he died in a hospice of an AIDS-related illness. His death certificate attributed the death to 'unknown natural causes' and listed his occupation as 'laborer' in the manufacturing industry."[28] Later, after an AIDS activist filed a complaint, the cause of death was corrected, but the lie about his work was left standing.

This deception about the cause of death has not, according to Sipe, been confined to this one case. "One of the difficulties in gathering facts," he suggests, "is that the causes of death and the occupations are often changed on priests' death certificates. It is very common, for example, for priests to be listed as 'travel agents.' "[29] If the person's occupation is changed, the statistic vanishes, but the truth does not.

The last humiliation for these good men, almost all of whom had no idea of the awakening to their sexual identity and needs that would occur after their ordination, takes place in their being defrocked as they are lowered into their graves, their life's work with all its good denied and distorted, the truth of their personalities disguised, as the official Church exhibits its corruption in what can only be described as its choosing the darkness over the light.

This last and highest treason abuses the personhood of everyone who agrees to it or becomes an accomplice for "the good of the Church." This final shaming of the dead for fear that they might yet cry out against such official asexual hypocrisy explains to us why, even as a new century begins, the wound of sexuality remains unhealed. Nothing can heal when those called to cure it choose instead to reinfect it every day.

14

WHAT WOUNDS ARE THESE?

✝

THAT THE OFFICIAL CHURCH may be found wounded and corrupt—and perhaps perversely corrupting—as it manipulates sexuality to its own end of controlling men and women is shocking, but by no means novel. The human side of the Church has lived up to its downside throughout history. We cannot back away, as some of the best of believers have been bidden to do, and veil our eyes "for the good of the Church." Instead, we take up the scripture's mythic task: to name correctly every living thing, including the creatures crowded into the hold of the ark, blind from lack of light, sick from fouled air, the deck above them rumbling from the lowing and baying of their wild drive to break free.

We identify and thereby free the penned animals, or we allow those who would be their masters to seize us and be our masters as well. Beneath their grave and affected piety, institutionally absorbed Churchmen savor their exercise of power over human intimacy much as other men do secret sexual fantasies. They view personality as divided, sectioned off as is the ark itself, and find healthy heterosexuality so threatening that it must be broken by the misery of the passage, made to seem unhealthy and so brought under their sway. Thus, the wounded Church as Institution indulges its taste for domination, its demands for submission, and its rationalization of the gratifications its officials take as lonely men do in the last rows of a darkened theater.

But this is not the whole Church, this barque of Peter made

into the *Amistad*, with tiers of decks to match its vision of the higher and lower ranking, the greater and lesser worthiness, between and within humans. Neither is this the Church to which most Catholics, whether they call themselves progressive or traditional, belong. That the administrative Church should be such a devouring bureaucracy is only one aspect of the Church as Mystery, the Church as a People of God, a communion of human relationships rather than a Henry James men's club, membership by invitation only. The Church as Mystery is fundamentally a home for sinners, in which lives a family ever ready to make room even for prodigal children. It has never been the eternal Skull and Bones prepared to blackball or expel the unwanted.

Mystery indexes our lives in a hundred ways each day, even in the events we give no name to, in every coming and going, in the small losses and the even smaller gains, in the little deaths we suffer and conquer, as we do time itself, without becoming self-conscious, through loving each other. Religion, as Pope John XXIII understood, appeals first to the imagination and not, as Pope John Paul II regularly insists, to the will. The Catholic Church is not, therefore, the Institution that we read and hear so much about, that great vessel of conquest, still powered by the wind, seeing us as it sees itself, so stratified as to be a miniature of God's hierarchical creation.

This function of this Church as Institution is to serve rather than to dominate the Church as Mystery. It injures itself on the sharp edges of the hierarchical divisions that it presses into humanity, tearing apart what it should be making whole. As a result, instead of making peace with sexuality—remembering that peace is not related to perfection—men and women are set at odds with sexuality and with themselves. This sexual wound weeps still because of the divided model that forces it open as a clamp does an incision. The symptoms and problems that we will now examine are not recognized as manifestations of this fundamental wound, but they are true if unsuspected effects of this great original wound to the integrity of human personality, that mother of all wounds estranging human beings from their humanity, setting them at odds with their sexuality, pitting male against female, intellect against emotion, imagination against will, and the spirit ever and always against the flesh.

BLEEDING THE MYSTERY: THE PRIEST SHORTAGE

These themes obsess the Church as Institution, which makes dangerous double-or-nothing wagers with history by betting, for example, that it can keep women and married men out of the priesthood and still supply the sacraments to its members. To preserve this embargo on healthy heterosexuality and to spare itself from that apparently most threatening of tasks—forming mature relationships with women—the Church as Institution is willing to take its losses and regroup around a core of what we might term Institutionalites, those who are gratified within themselves, and often rewarded within this ecclesiastical universe, by surrendering both their wills and their imaginations, their souls, we might say, "for the good of the Church." One day they may understand what bewilders them now: the more they draw down the stocks of the authoritarianism they misdefine as authority, the more it misfires or fails. It is truly hard for such anointed bureaucrats to see how self-defeating are their choices, for as they energetically prop up a royal model as dead as the Romanovs, they press on the unhealed wound that, like a leech set on a lesion, bleeds the sacramental heart of the Church as Mystery.

A revealing example is found in what is termed the priest shortage, the dramatic decline in the number of male applicants for the seminary in the United States and other Western countries since the end of the Brick and Mortar period. By extension, this also encompasses the steep drop in the number of women and men who enter religious life. This grave challenge is chronically misperceived and mishandled by the manager bishops of the official

Church, who have been reluctant to admit that it is a problem at all. What is so threatening in the elements of this crisis that Church officials defend themselves against examining it thoroughly and identifying it correctly?

VOCATIONAL CRISIS AS SEXUAL CRISIS

The shortfall in seminary applicants; the resignation of many priests to marry; the dying off of the last of the Brick and Mortar generation of clerics; the unsettled and unsettling efforts of Pope John Paul II to effect a final solution to the women's ordination question; the "don't ask, don't tell, don't dare to find out" approach to the issue of priest pedophilia and clerical homosexuality; the papal stance, abstract but absolute, on a birth-control teaching clearly not received in the discernment of conscientious Catholics; the righteous restoration of sex to its proper gravity as a sin by aspirant seminarians, about whose own psychosexual maturity serious questions remain unanswered—the common denominator of all these manifestations is conflicted and unexamined sexuality. The priest shortage is not, therefore, a discrete problem but a function of this cluster of symptoms that speak plangently of the unhealed sexual wound in institutional Catholicism.

Although this crisis has been building for two generations, the country's Catholic bishops at their meeting in Milwaukee in June 2000, "for the first time as a body . . . confronted the priest shortage and began discussing strategies to combat it."[1] Not only has the decline been denied, but its many indications have been routinely misinterpreted or so forced into the vocabulary of the Institution that their significance has been buried in an unmarked grave.

A study prepared for the American bishops by the Center for Applied Research in the Apostolate at Georgetown University reveals that in 1965, 58,132 priests served 46.6 million Catholics in the United States. Now 46,709 priests, a decline of 20 percent, serve 62.4 million Catholics, an increase of 34 percent. At present, the average age of priests who belong to a diocese is fifty-seven, while that of priests who belong to religious orders, such as the Jesuits, is sixty-three. Almost 27 percent of the nation's parishes either share a pastor with another church or do not have one at all. Of the 46,700 priests in the country, only 27,000 serve in parishes. The greatest revelations sometimes cling to the bottom of the cup, for if 433 priests are ninety years of age or older, only 298 are younger than thirty.

The institutional response is as classic as that of the World War I generals who found that the once reliable strategy of massive assaults by troops failed in this new and unfamiliar conflict and stalled completely in the mud of Flanders fields. Their unimaginative solution was to repeat the error that they denied and throw even greater numbers of troops at each other, turning the trenches into graves for millions of young men. The bishops' unimaginative solution to the declining number of priests is not to try to understand the sexual roots of the problem that cry out for examination but to accommodate themselves to sexual corruption, to try to survive with fewer priests by decreasing sacramental service to their people: 13 percent of dioceses are closing parishes, and 42 percent are reducing the number of masses. Eighty-six percent of dioceses expect a major increase in ministry by laypeople over the next ten years. In short, a full-blown crisis is being handled not by cleansing the temple but by reducing the times it is available for prayer.

Perhaps more instructive are the observations offered by some of the bishops. Archbishop Theodore McCarrick, then of Newark, New Jersey, and now of Washington D.C., realistically announced that his current supply of 544 priests would soon drop to 192 because of deaths, retirements, and the ordination of only about twelve priests a year. Another bishop offered a vintage example of institutional denial by suggesting that "we stop talking about the shortage of priests. . . . It gives a bad impression . . . [and] discourages the laity." In what can only be termed a unique managerial insight, auxiliary Bishop Thomas Curry of Los Angeles, noting that some parishes in his area serve eighteen thousand households, wondered whether the Church should work at bringing back Catholics who have dropped away: "If we invite them back, what in heaven's name will we do with them?"[2]

ANYTHING BUT THE TRUTH

This study, commissioned by and for the bishops, was handicapped from within from the start. For there is no lack of interest in ministry within Catholicism; therefore, ample resources exist to solve the illusory vocational shortage and to supply the full sacramental needs of Catholics. The findings reveal, for example, that ministry is currently being carried out by 30,000 lay or religious, with another 30,000 in training, along with 13,000 deacons, 150,000 schoolteachers, and 25,000 lay associates of religious orders. Toledo bishop James Hoffman was one of only four bishops who raised the issue of ordaining other candidates, noting that he "rarely attends a meeting where ideas about extending the priesthood to women and married men or inviting back resigned priests do not come up for discussion."[3]

According to Bryan Froehle, who worked on the research, the "bishops had deliberately omitted questions about ordination," saying that they already had enough data "saw no reason to include it in the survey."[4] In other words, they ruled out an examination of ways in which the sacraments could be provided to Catholics by, for example, raising the ordained deacons to the priesthood, a move that would require no change in Church law and would supply thousands of well-trained priests overnight. In other words, the core of the problem is not so much a shortage of people willing and able to minister as it is a shortage of clerics, which is a function of extensive, interrelated and unresolved sexual conflicts. That, however, is denied because it is too threatening for the Institution to examine. An inadequate solution, perhaps sinful in its failure to provide pastoral service to ordinary people, is preferred and, indeed, proposed.

SACRAMENTA PROPTER HOMINES

During World War II Archbishop Francis J. Spellman of New York often visited the battlefronts in his role as vicar for the American Armed Forces. At one station he encountered a priest chaplain who was saying mass more than a dozen times a day for the hard-pressed troops, a practice then well beyond canonical provisions. When Spellman was asked about what seemed an irregularity, he answered with the theological aphorism that summed up a profound pastoral insight, *sacramenta propter homines*, which we may translate as "the sacraments are for human beings." In other words, no letter of the law could nullify its spirit, in this case, to give spiritual nourishment to the troops.

This pastoral sense is strangely absent from the American bishops' approach to the priest shortage. Denying the sacraments to Catholics, the regular provision of which is the most serious obligation of these bishops, does not seem so bad to them when they put it into an invented setting of other explanations for the priest shortage. Church officials blame the age itself, with its sensual and monetary allures, for the drop of interest in entering the seminary. Others believe that the past will return, that everything will "settle down" and things will be as they once were. So they emphasize the need to pray more for vocations or a return to the kind of recruitment campaigns that gleaned so abundantly from the fields white for the harvest during the Brick and Mortar years.

In a corollary, bishops appear to be grateful for any applicants to the priesthood and have postponed a serious examination of the gay subculture that has been identified in contemporary life in seminaries and in the priesthood itself.[5] This is the *Beau Geste* approach, as exemplified in the old drama about troops beleaguered in the desert: propping dead men on the battlements as long as they appear to fill the niches of the legionnaires defending the fort.

What is at stake in the official way of perceiving this present reality of a vanishing priesthood? Nothing less than the sacramental life of Catholicism, which is its central element and the symbol system through which the Church as Mystery understands itself and speaks to its members and to the world. The crisis is, therefore, far more than a priest shortage. It is rather a *sacramental* crisis in which the Eucharist and the other vital sacraments are being denied to Catholics because the official Church has made a clear statement about its sexually rooted priorities: it would rather suffer a decrease in the availability of the sacraments than examine the nucleus of the conflicted sexuality that lies beneath the divided view of personality that so shakily supports its exaltation of virginity as a condition for functioning in the priesthood.

Organizational leaders betray a fear less of a shortage of priests than a shortage of clerics, that is, the counterpart castrati who accept sexual maiming not for any legitimate scriptural reason but to sacrifice, with little understanding of themselves or what they are really doing, their sexuality in an act of submission to other males, who are often equally unaware of themselves, of the hurt they do themselves, or of the needs they gratify within the web of these sexually charged institutional dynamics.

The leaders who cannot or will not survey the sexual dynamic that governs their isolation, and preservation at all costs, of a putatively virginal clergy are themselves wounded Grail Kings. Even as the American bishops gather to speak of this subject, their most obvious characteristic is discomfort with the question and their lack of ease with themselves in discussing it. They may long for the comfort of their once ubiquitous mothers, but that world, and that stage and style of early-life relationship, cannot sustain them forever. They do not think of "forever," however, but only of getting through this season, this year, this papacy. Here and now, in this castle that bespeaks power and achievement, they can find no place to sit or stand or lie down, for their desperate wound is aggravated rather than relieved by these moves, each of which is an adjustment to, rather than a cure for, the sexual wound most of them deny and few of them want to inspect and about which everyone else is afraid to ask them.

This so-called priest shortage is, therefore, the evidence of a profound institutional problem. The underlying element is that of the unresolved psychosexual impasse, the unhealed wound that is the connective between raising celibacy/virginity as a host in a gilded institutional monstrance and the problems that radiate from that very structure: The official Church's refusal to ordain married men or allow ordained men to marry; the implacable refusal even to discuss the ordination of women even though most ministry is carried out by women; the refusal to examine the sexual pathology in the celibate priesthood, which is revealed in pedophilia and other problems; the acceptance of homosexual students in the seminary system and of homosexuals in the priesthood despite the overstated and utterly unjustified insistence that they harbor an "objective disorder"; the suppression of pastoral ministries to gays and the transparently sexual demands made on individuals such as Sister Jeannine Gramick—that they "submit in silence," as women must in every immature male fantasy; the scapegoating of properly laicized priests, driven with their unworthiness into the wilds to atone for their heterosexuality, along with the women who are their wives, made to seem scarlet, as is the love they share, by the official refusal to acknowledge their existence; the systematic official gathering of data to demonstrate that no priest with a true vocation, but only the fraudulent and the mad, has ever sought laicization; the American bishops' inability to form a national policy on pedophilia among the clergy and their new tough, law- and insurance-based rejection of plaintiffs' claims and their crusadelike readiness to countersue them if they seek redress for being sexually violated by priests; the centerpiece of this strategy, the abandonment of the priest himself as an "independent contractor" to whom the institution, to whose bishop he is committed by obedience and on whose structure he is totally dependent, owes nothing. Thus is preserved the terrible fiction that the Institution has never made a mistake; thus its false conscience is maintained, and against every wish of the hearts of loyal Catholics, an image of institution as whited sepulchre rises as icy as an Arctic dawn in the imagination.

SEXUAL TENSIONS BENEATH THE SURFACE

The shortage of priests can be understood and addressed only if this broken family of related issues is studied and their unifying common denominator of strife-ridden sexuality is acknowledged and dispassionately explored. The official Church, failing to understand operationally the unity of human personality, fails also to see the unity of these issues. Pope John Paul II perceives no relationship among these issues except as fodder for the dissent that he wishes to eliminate. Yet it is the very hierarchical nature of the Church—which, in his judgment, "flows from its essence and nature"—that perpetuates the graded divisions in human personality that prevent the wound in sexuality from healing. If the official Church could admit its own discomfort with sexuality, as inseparable as the blood from the wound, and could take even a small, undefended, and therefore healthy step toward understanding it, the priest shortage would vanish, the sacramental life of the Church as Mystery would be guaranteed, and respect for the authority of the Institutional Church would begin to rise immediately.

PRO-CHOICE AND PRO-LIFE

The unaccepted sexual tension beneath subjects that, like the priest shortage, appear on the surface to be unconnected and unrelated to it may also explain the explosive and divisive nature of another sexually related subject, abortion. The U.S. Supreme Court has translated abortion into the language of law, finding "emanations," as the late Justice William O. Douglas put it, of its guarantee within a "right to privacy" in the Constitution. This is, in the secular sphere, an example of reframing an issue so that what really takes place in the act of abortion need never be examined. We are familiar with the public-relations phrase that blurs the essential transaction even more, "the right to choose," one of the great unfinished clauses in American culture, since it omits the object of choice by glorifying the act of choice as an end in itself.

What lies beneath this legalistic way of dealing with abortion if not some greater dynamism among women to gain what they awkwardly describe as "control of their own bodies" when they mean, at a deeper level, to break free of domination by men? Perhaps the climate of the abortion debate would improve if there were more focus on this basic undergirding and still far from resolved issue. How is this related to the Institutional Church's need to heal its sexual wound before it can deal with other seemingly unrelated issues?

The possibility of women becoming priests supplies us with a likely hypothesis. Beneath this search for ordination for women, we come upon the same tension that lies beneath the abortion issue. The unresolved reality—an aspect of the sexual woundedness of the Church—is whether women will ever be respected as equal to men and overcome the domination by men, whose signature has been branded so deeply into the ecclesiastical organizational tree that it seems as natural to those who tend it as the grain of the wood itself.

Why, we may ask again, in an age when the sacramental life that constitutes the Church as a religious mystery is imperiled, can the Pope adamantly and almost angrily refuse to ordain women and, beyond that, try to stamp out all discussion of the subject and make complete acceptance of and compliance with his views a crucial litmus test that must be passed by any man who wants to be named a bishop? What explains what might without exaggeration be described as protesting too much, if not some deeper drive, rationalized as maintaining divinely ordered male hierarchy but more complex and more explicitly sexual than that?

Is the muscular reluctance to admit women to orders justified by the scriptural and theological reasons that the Pope invokes? We have seen that these arguments are as insubstantial as they are unpersuasive to the majority of Catholics, whose judgment is not without its own theological significance as the implementation of the Church's "gift of reception." We may briefly observe, before we speculate on this question, the history of chronic male fear of and suppression of women by the Institutional Church.

OF MAKING SAINTS AND HOLY HUNGERS

Professors Rudolph Bell and Donald Weinstein have explored the male domination of the Institutional Church, which, like a tree a thousand years rooted, seems always to have been there. This is reflected in the way in which, to bolster itself after the Reformation, the official Church took unto itself the naming of saints. Pope John Paul II has followed the same path as, early in the year 2000, he set a *Guinness Book*–like mark for having canonized more saints than all previous popes combined. While it is clear that he wants to emphasize the good example that holy people offer, he has other reasons for making saints as well.

Bell and Weinstein track the Institutional Church's studied and steady efforts to control women throughout history.[6] Barring them from the priesthood is only part of a long-term program that we can understand better, for example, in the way the Institution reacted, in the light of the Reformation's emphasis on the individual, to the threat of free-floating holy people, such as Francis of Assisi, whose lives and works were independent and therefore beyond the control of the organized Church. The Assisis of the time were as unsettling as the Luthers of a later period to the Institution. The official Church instinctively took control of holiness as any multinational corporation does a subsidiary that threatens to break away on its own.

"The early sixteenth century," the researchers write, ". . . was a time of crisis for the cult of saints. Saints had embodied religious innovation and given direction to public piety for the preceding three hundred years, but with the Reformation the traditional structures of belief and organization came under fire as never before."[7] If burgeoning Protestantism challenged hierarchical divisions by eliminating the need for mediation with God through ecclesiastical structures, saints like Francis ignited the imagination of Catholics, offering them a way of holiness that was outside the keeping of the Institutional Church.

"The response of that Counter-Reformation church," according to Bell and Weinstein, ". . . was to assume increasing control of cult formation and then to make it less accessible to popular and spontaneous religious enthusiasm." The Institution yearned for control because "the saints challenged the clerical hierarchy on several fronts," not only because their holiness was a living reproach to many clerics but because of other crucial issues, especially the development of their own beliefs around a certain saint but also in more mundane matters, such as "the mongering of relics" that could "set monasteries and towns against each other." There were also "local communities driving for autonomy [who] used cults of local saints to enhance their standing as well as to focus civic patriotism. Some of the more powerful, like Venice, even had pretensions to religious authority independent of and equal to that of the papacy."[8]

CONTROL OF THEIR OWN BODIES

Rapidly regaining control was an immediate institutional objective that, as it was carried out, had a number of negative effects on women. Their ambitions within the Church were curtailed, and lacking this opportunity, the vise of their domination by a patriarchal society tightened. Not the least of the areas needing control was the making of saints to ensure that devotion to them also meant devotion to the Institution. The proportion of males declared saints began to grow enormously in relationship to the number of females who were canonized.

The process of recognizing and officially sponsoring saints came under the effective supervision of the Institution and was made to serve and support what Bell terms, in a related work, the "hierarchical male prelacy."[9] The counterattack matches exactly the tactic of making saints employed so prodigally by Pope John Paul II. What needed to be brought back under control then was, as now, "the lay piety, with its emphasis on individual responsibility, that . . . had flourished within mother church's bosom and that now had become its mortal enemy."[10]

Under the weight of the domination that characterized women's life inside and outside the Church, a remarkable response developed whose symbolic meaning helps us understand that women want to break free of ecclesiastical control in our own time. The modes of feminine spirituality then undertaken were, according to Bell, disguised strivings to reassume control of their own lives. One of these tactics, extreme fasting—practiced, among others, by Saint Catherine of Siena and Saint Clare of Assisi—flows on the current of sexual energy crackling beneath the question of ordaining women and allows us to see the relationship of the latter with the question of abortion.

Extreme fasting gave women a way to escape the otherwise total male clerical control of their lives and to gain some autonomy for themselves. Dominated by the patriarchal Church and State in every other way, these women could challenge and frustrate their confessors and ecclesiastical authority through controlling their own eating habits, through, in other words, claiming control—as women do in a similar symbolic way in our time—over their own bodies. As Bell notes, "It . . . became evident that woman's holiness was the consequence of sacrifice and willpower, no longer could the female saint be viewed simply as the receptacle of divine grace, always in need of male guidance. Woman as object, possessed of no interior spirituality, gave way to woman as subject, creator of her destiny."[11]

One may trace a series of these symbolic efforts by women within the Church to break free of male domination. As the Church labored to get extreme fasting under control, women turned to other methods, such as bizarre forms of illness that enabled these women to remain in bed most of the time, and therefore effectively beyond masculine control. Men could not follow them there any more than they could into the universe of body control exemplified in fasting. Nor, in later centuries, could they follow women who carved out a sphere of independent self-control, as Mother Cabrini did in early-twentieth-century Chicago by her enormous zeal for charitable works. The late Mother Teresa of Calcutta supported the Institution but achieved effective independence from it through her saint's life of service to the dying poor. No ecclesiastic, not even the Pope, could or did attempt to tell Mother Teresa what to do. She told them, and in a remarkable example of how the clergy were intimidated by a woman, they could only agree, as they did, with any proposals she made. A different kind of woman, Mother Angelica, outwitted America's bishops as she preempted them on controlling a Catholic television station that she has turned into the Eternal Word Network, a haven for pre–Vatican II theology and devotion. While she, too, supports the Institution, the entrepreneurial Mother Angelica operates, to the frustration of bishops who must match that of their sixteenth-century predecessors, outside their effective influence.

We may observe the similarity of the sexual dynamic beneath the symbolic efforts of the saints of the Middle Ages to shake off male domination with the current struggles for the equality of women. Among the latter we cannot fail to identify abortion now described as almost exactly like the fasting efforts of Saint Catherine of Siena, as women taking unto themselves an issue in which men cannot easily follow, the control of their own bodies.

IF THE POPE ORDAINED WOMEN . . .

Suppose, instead of restating his emotional opposition to women's ordination, the Pope were to change his mind and approve it instead. Suppose he did not go that far but merely stated that he would welcome and attend carefully to a resumption of the theological investigations of the ordination of women that he ruled out a few years ago.

Enormous banner headlines would follow around the globe because, without fully understanding it, millions of people, including non-Catholics, would grasp that something momentous was under way, something far more significant than the surface chatter sure to follow about what would happen to rectories and other practical considerations. This announcement would, in fact, strike the chains off the dynamic of control of women by men that lies, even more closely than the destiny of the vulnerable unborn, close to the heart of the abortion debate.

One must not shrug off fetal life as of no consequence, but if the unborn are to be saved, it will only follow a recognition that the true issue is that of the liberation of women from the patriarchal control of men. In fact, the full recognition of the unborn as humans invested fully with the rights of persons cannot be achieved until the full recognition of women as humans invested fully with the rights of persons takes place within the official Church. The question is not only "Is the fetus a person?" but also "Is the woman a person?"

The pro-life position would be enhanced, as would the cause of women everywhere in the world, if the Pope recognized women as equal persons by reopening the question of their ordination to the priesthood. The abortion-rights debate is described reflexively as a "struggle" because many women feel that male institutions, including the Church, are pitted against them, that men have so long dominated women in matters of doctrine and discipline that overseeing their intimate lives seems natural, indeed, supernatural, to them, the way God meant things to be.

TRANSACTIONS BENEATH THE SURFACE

Many women who adopt the pro-choice position are not so much in favor of abortion as they are against what they perceive as their historical oppression by men. The resulting impulse for long-denied equality has expressed itself in dozens of ways in such movements as seeking the vote; entrance into, and equal pay with men in, the professions; freedom from workplace sexual harassment; and, like it or not, awkwardly or not, the right to make their own decisions about their reproductive lives.

The term *struggle* could be applied to all of these, for none of these efforts to be recognized as equal has been achieved without overturning the tables in the temple of the all-male culture. In it we sense the *ponos*, the Greek for *toil* that ever accompanies the *pathos* or *pain*, which together constitute the components of every agonized effort by women to author their own lives—intellectual, social, professional, or sexual.

An institution run by men that refuses even to discuss women priests on the basis of arguments with which its own theologians disagree sparks dissension and argument on the conscious level. On the plane of true transaction, it powerfully, almost blindly, reasserts men's control over women. No matter the flowing reassurances offered about the dignity of women uttered in sermons, women receive the closed-captioned version: Stay in your place, and we will revere you.

How, we may ask, could women react otherwise when, even as

they exalt an abstract and sexless feminine, male clerics tell women, even at the poorest and most shadowed ends of the earth, that they may not choose contraceptive services even if they suffer rape or incest. Men who so confidently make such judgments betray themselves in a way in which they cannot even imagine themselves, as oppressive and controlling about experiences they will never have.

Asserting the right to choice is, therefore, for many women, a protest against an almost infinite array of masculine controls and defenses. Were Church leaders to welcome a theological review of women's ordination, they would tell women more than that this option might be open to them. They would communicate what they aver abstractly, that women are their equals. Were this move real instead of merely political, the struggle, the *ponos* and the *pathos,* beneath the surface of all questions related to women, including abortion, would diminish. An enormous blow would also be struck against the extensive oppression of women still found in slavery, forced prostitution, forced abortions, and other practices throughout the world.

The pro-life campaign will never completely succeed on the conscious level until the Church as an Institution addresses the issues that the Church as Mystery can easily accommodate. The arguments against women's ordination will be experienced as arguments against women, and evidence of an unhealed sexual wound, until male ecclesiastics identify that wound as their own and begin to heal it by surrendering their attempts to define and master the spiritual and physical destinies of women.

WHAT IS IT THAT AILS YOU?

✝

WHAT IS DESCRIBED AS a priest shortage in the United States is, therefore, less a failure of faith than a symptom of the unhealed sexual wound in the Institutional Church, that Grail castle of our guiding myth, in which the vast bureaucracy, reflecting the spell cast by the ancient story's court protocol, makes itself mute for fear that it may suffer loss by saying the wrong thing in the presence of the king. Garbed in the robes, and even bearing the titles, of court life, these bureaucrats cannot imagine, much less ask, the simple human question that, by its being spoken aloud, brings wholeness to this wound that weeps with the tears of all men and women who have suffered it. Speak but the word, and my spirit will be healed.

The words *healing* and *wholeness* are virtual twins in the family of language. They signify the same thing: the making whole that is healing, the healing that brings wholeness. They are the linguistic genomes for *health* and *healthy*, as well as for *holy*. The primary meaning of the latter, we learn, refers to whatever " 'must be preserved whole or intact, that cannot be transgressed or violated,' which would support its relationship to Old English *hal*, whole."[1]

These ideas of whole, healthy, and holy are the foundation for the thesis of this book—that once the wholeness, or integrity, of personality is shattered, as by its division into warring elements of flesh and spirit, mind and body, intellect and emotions, then what is holy is indeed "transgressed or violated" and what is healthy is confused with and infected by what is unhealthy. What happens when persons are forced for centuries to accept a distorted model of themselves? Think of those held for generations as slaves, the idea that they were property, not persons, that they were unworthy and inferior to whites, bred and beaten into them? We can understand how their sense of themselves and of their integrity—of being whole, healthy, and free—is thereby damaged and only slowly made whole. So it is with men and women, the idea of their being uneasy amalgams of flesh and spirit having been bred and beaten into them for generations. To their damaged sense of wholeness and health comes this wound that cannot be healed by those whose idea of curing it is to prevent it from closing.

The Church as Institution, that great organization whose sole purpose is to serve the Church as Mystery, cannot bring healing to others until it first heals its broken notion of the human person. Nor can it be holy, or even recognize and affirm what is holy in the world, until it purges itself of unhealthy ideas about men and women and supplants these ideas with healthy ones instead. What is holy, as with what is healthy and whole, chooses sunlight over darkness and fresh air over the odors of tombs and sealed-off centuries. What is healthy can also withstand any test by human experience; what is unhealthy fails the test of human experience, and its corrupted wholeness is easily diagnosed as such.

THE PASTORAL RESPONSE

It is time for this Church as Institution to ask—or to allow somebody uninfected by the virus of bureaucracy to ask—that question whose healthy simplicity cleans out and heals this long-festering wound: What is it that ails you? The very placing of the question is sacramental, that is, in itself it brings about what it symbolizes. For it is not a command seeking control. It is rather a question alive with authority, that human energy enlarging the other, that authority of the Word itself, made flesh to reveal our glory—and that of our world—to ourselves.

Here we come upon words that serve the Word and whose meaning is central to our understanding the function of the Church as Mystery. For *cure* and *care* share the Latin root of *cura*, which means "care," "concern," "attention," or "management." These are in turn related to *curiosity,* which means to be "full of care" and, of course, "eager to know." Those not eager to learn the truth of the world cannot care for the world, for they are dominated by fear instead of moved by love. Those who love always want to learn more about their beloved. The truly curious take care of the world through learning ever more deeply the truths that constitute its truth.

We thereby define nothing less than the pastoral response, that mode through which the Church as Mystery replies to, mediates, and heals all that is broken in human life. This capacity to tend the wounded in the zigzag trenches of a tragically divided battleground is what makes *the* Church *a* Church, a Mystery as a family is, or a friendship, the birth of children, or the bonds of love, a Mystery and no bureaucracy at all.

How striking that the central and centralizing bureaucracy of the Institutional Church is termed the Curia, a word that is first cousin to *cure* and *care.* Even if we concede the Curia's task to be management, this collage of bureaus can accomplish that only by being *full of care* for and *eager to know* about the world. These are healthy and generous impulses, but how often in our survey of cur- ial actions do we find that fear of the truth overshadows seeking the truth, followed by an eagerness to control—indeed, to suppress rather than to encourage—knowing, so that officials limit what can be known of the human and the world, and characterize that as evil far more than as creation's glory. The Curia's consuming concern for the survival of the Church as Institution takes precedence over its support and service of the Church as Mystery.

This curial attitude of caution about creation was expressed perfectly by a cardinal archbishop when he insisted that Vatican II documents spoke of the Church's "limited accommodation to the world in view of evangelizing it."[2] This highly conditional sentiment can be made only by someone standing aside from the world, emphasizing the division between it and the Church and the correlated division that stripes human personality as well. This expression is, at its core, hostile to creation and, as we shall see, essentially nonsacramental.

The Church as Mystery embraces the world, the erring rather than the perfect world, by being full of care for it, encouraging learning about it, unsurprised by the sinfulness and imperfection that mar all creation, including us humans. In short, the pastoral Church. In the Vatican II document *The Church in the Modern World,* this Church addresses a world "capable of doing what is noble and what is base, disposed to freedom and slavery, progress and decline, amity and hatred."[3] Yet it affirms that "the Spirit of the Lord fills the whole world" and that we find God "in the events, the needs, and the desires" that humankind and the Church share together."[4]

The Church does not, therefore, thunder a judgment at the world, "This is what is wrong with you," but rather asks Parzival's question, a true pastor's question, "What is it that ails you?" This is how we cure, this is how we take care of, this is how we are curious about all of creation. As Christian Catholics we are not expected to make the world perfect but to help it heal its wounds and achieve holiness by being healthy. In no concern is this pastoral response more significant than in relationship to human sexuality.

BRICK, MORTAR, AND CONCRETE

When the Institutional Church addresses creation in its own business language of canon law, it is really talking only to itself. The Church as Mystery, however, speaks creation's own language through its sacraments. During the Brick and Mortar Age, when the rumble of cement trucks counterpointed the rumble of the church organ, canon law, the pragmatic tongue of "how" and "why" and "who's in charge" regulations, all but made a dead language of the sacraments. This triumph of can-do canon law was, by the middle of the twentieth century, so complete that the Liturgy had been reduced to rubrics, the finely detailed, indeed, obsessive laws for celebrating the sacraments—laws that were to the sacraments' essence as the menu is to the meal. Like curates out of Trollope, officials offered judgments on the physical composition of the flour in the bread and the grape in the wine rather than insights into the spiritual significance of their transformation into the body and blood of Christ in the Eucharist.

At the high point of the vocation boom of Brick and Mortar times—when, in a miniaturization of hierarchy, Latin masses were rattled off by priests elevated above and with their backs to the people—the Church's sacramental sense was badly atrophied. Not only did canon lawyers dominate the Liturgy but they were also the principal teachers of a rote and by-the-numbers moral theology. This emphasis on law over spirit fortified the official Church's orientation toward divided personality and, therefore, toward acts that could be enumerated in the confessional, where priests were instructed to ask of almost everything, "How many times?" The sacramentality that focuses on the activity of *whole* persons was obscured by a blizzard of legalisms. A favorite maxim of canon lawyers of that heady period of practical achievement was "Keep the law, and the law will keep you."

This attitude had its application in the salient legalism in training for the priesthood. The *Seminary Rule,* an elaborate handbook with exact rules for everything from how to get out of bed in the morning to how to get back into it in the evening, was spoken of as "God's will," and conformity to it was the seminarian's way to sanctity. One cannot, however, employ brick and mortar as building materials without a preference for the concrete. Why else did it seem natural to speak of the "footings" and "foundations" of the spiritual life and of choosing the hefty stones of literalism and legalism to appeal to the will over the sacramental and the spiritual that speak to the imagination? Was this sacramental dissonance in the air that artists breathed when a writer of the period titled his novel *Christ in Concrete*?

AMERICANS, A SACRAMENTALLY DEPRIVED PEOPLE

Sacramentality—that pastoral radiance of symbols that illuminate the critical passages of human life—lost its voice but did not disappear during that era of building in which Catholic morality was blueprint-clear and, in Catholic folklore, it seemed natural for the Virgin Mary, in her many alleged appearances, usually to small children, to say, "Build me here a beautiful church." The sacramental, like the novelist's Christ, was, of course, to be found in concrete.

Yet, so faint had the voice become—this voice that did not scold but instead asked what ailed the world—that it could be heard not only in the Catholic culture but in all of American experience. Listen to Bobby encountering, in David Mamet's 1997 play, *The Old Neighborhood,* people from his past life. The "most haunting and original element," a reviewer wrote, "is its characters' fantasies of an alternative world, in which religion and family and erotic love have a formal enduring sustenance." They ache for what we recognize as sacramentality, for a place where people "are a dream of their environment. Here their loves are a joy. Where questions are answered with ritual." They long for practices, as one character says, in which the "sorrows of years is condensed, do you see, into a *ceremony.* And then it is over."

Listen in real life at "one of the growing array of new rituals that women and men are creating to help them cope with the loss of a pregnancy, a loss that many . . . feel is not understood or acknowledged by family, friends, health care workers and religious leaders."[5] People want to give a name to and symbolize events that the culture, anxious for "closure," wants to forget or pretend never happened. These range from death to divorce and explain the appearance of sympathy cards designed to recognize and, at least in a small way, heal such nameless wounds. We find the loss of sacrament in the sacrament substitute of these cards that attempt to ask, "What is it that ails you?"

The mightiest witness to our cultural sacramental deprivation debarks from Southampton every day in our imagination, on movie and television screens, in books, museum exhibitions, and souvenirs. We cannot get enough of the *Titanic*, for it is the great mythic symbol, a sacrament, if you will, of the now ended twentieth century. It symbolically re-enacts our rediscovery of the unity of the human race and of the collapse of the hierarchical social structures that had dominated the imagination and the political ordering of the world for thousands of years.

The RMS *Titanic* is a *sacramentum mundi*, a sacrament of our world, of our being booked together, the beggar at the gate with the once complacent rich man, as we hurry through unrelenting time toward our inexorable destiny. In mythology, the deep is always the unconscious. The North Atlantic deep has become a sacred place. Touch the *Titanic*, and you touch all of us. That is why we cannot stay away from its resting place and are drawn to the rites of its loss. The vessel's broken body, spread across its ocean floor altar, radiates sacramentality, of life entered into, of cowardice and bravery, of death encountered and new life found, of the hierarchical division of classes erased by a common fate. We need to visit the ship as pilgrims do a shrine; we need to meditate on and listen to its dishes and spoons, its men's hats and women's finery and its own rust-feathered hull because of our need for sacraments. Sacraments break us free of time. That is why the *Titanic*, symbol of the vanished hierarchical division of the universe and of our rediscovered unity of personality and human destiny, sails every day anew in our common imagination and why its mystery attracts us freshly, agelessly, inexhaustibly. It is *our* mystery.

SPLITTING SPIRITUALITY FROM RELIGION

Yet the *Titanic's* full mythological meaning has not yet entered our awareness. We get hints of it in the way we are drawn to it, and most religious leaders mumble only trite phrases over the waters about man's ill-placed faith in progress and the wickedness of pride. They do not see that in its death, the *Titanic* became a source of life for humanity, a sacrament in itself, as we say, of our world and our lives. Still, for the moment, it remains a spectacle, a great "subject," for most of us who have not yet understood how, far from disintegrating a mile and more down in the Atlantic, it lives, lights ablaze and music playing, in our own depths.

What we can see are the effects of the split that runs through the universe, that wound unhealed by the Church, that father of divisions that forces spirit and flesh apart and, as we can see in our own day, that divorces sacrament from life. As a result, spirituality has now been secularized and severed from religion as surely as the brain fibers in a lobotomy. This distinction is barely noticed by religious leaders who still inveigh against the secular world without realizing how, by losing their own sacramental sense, they have opened their tabernacles and temples to it. Can the world really be thought of as secular in itself, we may ask, or does it only appear that way to those who have lost their sacramental way of seeing things?

As psychologist Kenneth I. Pargament notes, religion is now thought of "as the organizational, the ritual, the ideological," while spirituality is associated "with the personal, the affective, the experiential, and the thoughtful."[6] As a result, "an individual can be spiritual without being religious and . . . religious without being spiritual."[7] Spirituality decoupled from any religious institution is the fulfillment of the nineteenth-century prophecy of the Impressionist painters who deliberately omitted institutions from their work except as studies of light, as in Monet's paintings of the cathedral facade at Rouen. Impressionist paintings are popular because they match the institutionless New Age religion, providing pleasant pseudospiritual, substitute sacramental experiences for the masses. In short, they are the sacramentary for a spirituality successfully separated from religion both as Institution and as true Mystery.

Saint Francis of Assisi no longer represents the sacramental vision of the world that is the best heritage of Institutional Catholicism. He is now patron of a politicized ecological movement that is faith enough—spirituality without religion—in a superficially sacramentalized world. What the official Church does not recognize is the role it has played in pressing its model of divided creation into the modern consciousness. The present separation of spirituality and religion arises and flows from that long-ago sundering at the headwaters of the one river of personality.

So, too, the neutering of robust sacramentality has led to its becoming a protoplasmic feature, a special effect, if you will, in the New Age religionless religion that is popular because it provides a feeling of faith to people without making any of the demands of faith on them. It promises resurrection here and now, death, like batteries, not included. The very blandness of the New Age is a sign of its vague and diffuse sexuality and of its lack, therefore, of vital and potent sacraments. Thus Saint Francis, emasculated by the official Church as it took control of him and his spirit, has been desexualized. Francis loved the earth but he is no longer earthy, he is called a "human" saint by those who made him unthreatening but less human by obliterating his sexuality. He is not a vigorous young Italian who loved and was loved by Saint Clare, but a desexualized icon in a world that likes the idea of sacraments but not their demand for personal engagement, for their being generative and broadly sexual in authoring growth in us.

DESEXUALIZING THE SACRAMENTS

What happens when an official Church wants to control its sacraments by controlling the sexuality of those who administer them so much that it desexualizes the sacraments as well by denying their potency—their celebration of the mystery of creation and Creator—and denying them to its people in order to preserve an emasculated male, and perhaps not wholly masculine, priesthood? Yet this is the course chosen by bishops who deal with a shortage of priests to celebrate the sacraments by reducing mass availability and substituting nonsacramental "Eucharistic services" combining scripture readings and the distribution of previously consecrated hosts to those who attend.

This is to respond to a loss of Sacrament with no sacrament at all but with a generalized, bland service little different from that offered in non-Catholic Churches. Bishops would blush at the thought that by such decisions, they confess their own impotence, their emasculation by officials higher than they who reveal their profound uneasiness with the intrinsically generative character of the sacraments by insisting—against history, scripture, and theology—that what must be preserved is a sexless male priesthood rather than sexually keyed sacraments themselves.

Such a position signals their limited understanding of, and surely their lack of ease with, the sexual elements of the sacramental life of the Church as Mystery. Why be surprised that one of the effects of this mesmerization with an all-male priesthood, ignoring or failing even to examine the implications of the pedophile distillate of celibate sexuality, is to awaken to a generation of sexually conflicted candidates for the priesthood and sexually problematic priests in parish ministry?

Solutions to the need for those who can celebrate the Eucharist for the Catholic community are at hand, of course, but the light of their healthiness—their embrace of the heterosexual principle of creation—causes the unhealthy to shield their eyes. Such men would have their people go sacramentally hungry—when did we see you hungry?—rather than allow a married man or a woman to offer the Eucharist. Those solutions are automatically ruled out, while simple ones, such as ordaining to the priesthood the thousands of well-trained deacons now in its service, are not actively being considered. Let the people eat cake.

This Institutional reluctance or inability to recognize the ill-formed and immature sexuality that is its inner motive makes controlling the sex of sacramental ministers more important than the provision of sacraments to the people. That is a sexual scandal—its homoerotic elements denied or suppressed but unmistakable to any healthy person—that is related to and fed by the same headwaters as the other sexual scandals connected with the priesthood.

PASCHAL MYSTERY/PASTORAL MYSTERY

The Church as Mystery survives even on the hardscrabble streets of the Church as an Institution and keeps alive within it a pastoral feeling for fallible human beings. The best part of the "old" Church, as some recall it in its hard Brick and Mortar stage, was not so much its claims to tower, unchanging, above time but its readiness to change itself, many times if necessary, to respond to human need, taking on all the hazards and limitations of time in the process. The official Church understood this pastoral capacity to put the rules aside, to forgive the sinner, to heal the wound, to accommodate to the human state as less than that of the angels, to stand with the discouraged and fight for the oppressed. The Paschal Mystery is lived in the Pastoral Mystery.

Indeed, the official Church was so aware that much of its pastoral service had to be done unofficially that it had a name for it: *Epikeia*, Greek for "act of justice," by virtue of which a pastor enjoyed freedom of judgment because a "law need not be obeyed when its observance would be detrimental to the common good or the good of individuals."[8]

Through this pastoral sense the Church as Institution makes room for Mystery not by judging the world and finding it wanting but by listening to the world and finding it needy. Through such pastoral intuitions, the Church blows on the embers of its sacramental feeling for the sinful human condition, keeping them aglow at the level, far from officialdom, where ordinary people then lived and live still. Its main work has never been to dominate but to serve the world. This is how the Church as an Institution makes way for the Church as Mystery to fulfill its coextensive mythic and sacramental functions. This lingering sacramental sensibility was the official Church's salvation, for through this opening, its pastoral work touched humankind. Pope John XXIII called Vatican II to emphasize this "pastoral" outreach to the world. His metaphors indicate that he did not want to tear down the institution but rather to open its windows to the currents and cries of the world that it had shut out for many decades.

In calling the council, John XXIII placed Parzival's question to the world, "What is it that ails you?" He had struck this pastoral tone from the moment of his election, and the world, so much of it hardened in heart toward a Vatican that had spoken to it largely with reproaches and rules, turned toward this new pope as people do to the first warm sun of spring. He had asked the pastoral question and thereby healed an old wound of separation. The world found him as his attendants did when they told him that the workers would look away and keep their distance when he walked in the papal gardens. "Why?" he asked. "I won't harm them."

John XXIII was a healthy man who did not relate to the world through defenses. Since he raised none, the people of the world could put theirs aside and, unafraid that he would take advantage of them, move closer to him, delighted to be subjects of his pastoral concern. John XXIII embodied authority (from *augere*, "to grow"), for he was committed to the growth of others to their full stature. And the world, including non-Catholics by the millions, offered him obedience (from *ob-audire*, "to listen to") by looking up from their preoccupations to listen to him. Through the council, the Church was not to preach to, much less scold, the world. It was to take a look at and reform itself, recovering its sacramental appreciation and celebration of creation and of all creatures. John was to be what the Jewish philosopher Hannah Arendt called him, "a Christian in the chair of Peter." His profound pastoral and deeply Catholic wish for the council was that its deliberations would "make the human sojourn on earth less sad."

There can be no simpler or more profound description of the mission of the Church as Mystery than, through its mythic sacramental presence, it should wash the bleeding feet and nurse the unhealed wounds of its pilgrim people. Of the latter, the wound in human sexuality includes every aspect of the vital human being, for, sexually wounded, it is thoroughly wounded in its human sense. How can it, wounded, not be confused, as it is, about love and sex and giving and enlarging new life? How can it, wounded, not be dizzied by it own painful compromises and abuses of its sexuality, these wounds that sometimes wear a sophisticated and sometimes a perverse mask? Are they not all evidence of the inner woe of human beings seeking to heal the division in their personality?

THE MYSTERY NEEDS AN INSTITUTION

The Paschal Mystery, that of the resurrection that triumphs over death, has been celebrated for centuries with Easter eggs. At one time, people thought that in the full moon that sets the date of both Easter and Passover, in the moon that is the symbol of time as the sun is of eternity, they could make out on its surface the face of a rabbit, our "man in the moon," all creatures subject to time, to dying and rising with the moon. In this ancient evocation of the mystery of time and eternity, the egg is linked with the mystery of creation on many levels—with time, the waning of powers, of loss, then, and death, too, but also with sex, potency, and the generation of life. New life pecks at and breaks through this fragile shell to enter time and the mystery of life. Resurrection, the Paschal Mystery, symbolizes this unshelling of ourselves as we break through the hull of sin, loss, and hurt, to new life.

The Paschal feast depends on an institution that understands, preserves, and celebrates these symbols for the believing community. The sacramental inventory must be stored in an institution that appreciates their fertility, their potency, their sacred symbolism of the pilgrimage of life. No individual can do what an institution does do when it does all this in remembrance of Jesus, from whose life and death the Church arose. The Church as Institution bears and safeguards what it may not understand, for it is itself the tabernacle where are stored our religious dreams, the storehouse of the symbols of life as Mystery. The most important of these are the sacraments.

Institutionless Christianity, that is, one in which small communities cut themselves free from an institution that has chosen self-preservation over dynamic sacramentality, may be understandable but is not, in the long run, a practical vehicle for a Church as Mystery. Neither John XXIII nor the Council Fathers envisioned a free-flowing, on-its-own Christianity as an alternative to the creaking windmill of the institution they wished to update so that it would turn with, rather than against, the rhythms of the world as it is, the vast Mystery of Creation in which our lives are set.

Vatican II wanted a reformed institution, but certainly an institution. One must remember that the Church's structure allowed it to survive during the half century when the Iron Curtain descended to leave many Catholic countries under control of communism. A recent book proposes that Catholicism outlasted liberal Protestantism during the long dark night of communist control of Eastern Europe precisely because of its structure and despite its flaws and failures.

Researchers Paul Zulehner of Vienna and Miklos Tomka of Budapest contend that in countries (East Germany and the Czech Republic) in which liberal Protestantism flourished before the communist takeover, atheism is now the dominant belief. "Communists wanted to privatize religion, to deprive it of its connection to an institution," Zulehner told the *National Catholic Reporter*. "Protestantism was more congenial to this aim because it is a much more individualistic approach, and liberal Protestantism especially . . . stresses the Protestant *Geist*, or 'spirit,' the cultural phenomenon of Protestantism, not attachment to a Church."[9]

On the other end, "religious affiliation is high in Poland, Croatia, and Romania . . . where the established Churches [Catholicism and Orthodoxy] have strong institutional structures closely tied to national identity. Believers remain a majority in the other Catholic nations of the region, such as Slovenia and Slovakia."[10] The reason is that "support systems formed by an attachment to an institution are critically important to keeping the faith alive," Zulehner says, "whether the context is Marxism or Western liberalism, 'You can't be a Christian alone in a post-Christian society.' "[11] It is easier to be a Christian, then, if an organized Church preserves and makes available religious symbols that recapitulate the mystery of living in time and longing for eternity. In short, the sacraments.

Whether this Cold War institutional strength will endure depends, according to Zulehner, on whether this institution that closed ranks against communism can take on the reforms of Vatican II, especially in training leaders among the laity who must take responsibility for bringing Catholic values into the public square of business, culture, and government.

LIVING THE MYSTERY

Living a Mystery and a Myth does not mean that we are watching a drama performed for us by others. Religion is neither a pageant or a passion play. Nor are we, despite the expectant feelings of the time, living in an intermission, that leaderless and anxious interlude in which playgoers wait for the curtain to rise on a second act that will resolve all the conflicts developed in the first act. Many Catholics live that way, however, waiting for a new papacy to solve their problems. Nor are we watching a revival that has been staged and updated many times in history. We are not spectators at any kind of performance. This mystery is a Liturgy whose theme is eternal; we are the protagonists; the drama is our life story; the experience is our own.

We are living a Mythic Mystery, not as Civil War re-enactors who rise from the battlefield at dinnertime and go home to watch television. No, something real enters our lives that parallels the "something new" that Vatican II sensed as entering human experience in general. In the company of all who author, rather than follow, a script about their lives, we are roused to the "waking consciousness," as Campbell describes the primary function of mythology, "to the *Mysterium tremendum et fascinans* of the universe *as it is*."[12] That is the Catholic sense that the institution, despite its flaws and failings, has never lost.

THE NEW ARK

Noah called the animals onto the ark, in the myth of the great flood, in sexual pairs. It was his charge, as it is now the Church's, to identify correctly those who make the voyage on whose passenger manifest we find sexuality and in whose cargo, the world's fertility, its possibilities for life.

That the sexual wound remains unhealed is infinitely regrettable because the Catholic Church, not letting the fierce doctrinal hand know what the forgiving pastoral hand is doing, still supports and understands so much that matches the reality, and answers the needs of, human nature—for example, generously forgiving weakness, failure, and sin. The energy of its tradition produced such figures as Pope John XXIII, who felt the pulse of hurt in the open wound during his own long close-up experience with the epidemic pain of the twentieth century. He knew how harsh the voice of the official Church could be when it thundered from a distance in a dead language, offering to spiritually hungry people Roman stones instead of the bread of life. But he also knew that it could rouse itself to do better.

To close the untended lesion, John startled the administrative Church by calling the pastoral Church together, bidding the world's bishops to come apart, to retreat from their much-loved paperwork, and to listen in the quiet to the new world that was being born freshly in the universe around them. In that interlude they were to recover the Church's true voice, its pastoral ability to address ever broken human experience directly and in depth. John called the bishops, we might say, to raise the *Titanic* spiritually rather than physically, by building a new ark that would have room for men and women, just as they are, human and sexual, bearers of fertility to the world and, perhaps, to the stars beyond.

HEALING THE WOUND

While the renewal of Vatican II is often remembered or reviled in terms of its ideas, arguments, or documents, it was not—and, indeed, is not—just an intellectual debate summed up in its minutes or its resolutions. The council's voyage was, and remains, pastoral. Through it, the Church looked at itself so that it might see and serve the world better. The council may be best understood as that period, on the very edge of the Space Age, during which the Church took time to heal itself so that it could heal the world's wounded. Its own wound could be healed as every wound is, from within, as John XXIII well knew.

Vatican II's purpose was not to press infertile regulations on the world. The council addresses itself, the living Church—we use the present tense to capture its dynamic, unfolding character—not just to its intellect but to its whole person, thereby respecting and restoring its unity and identifying its subject as the mystery of human personality, male and female, the mystery of being a people, a community of relationships, undeniably sexual in every sense. The living council meditates, as we must if we are to enter Mystery, not on an abstract God or a philosophical First Mover, but on the human experience in which we encounter God, that vital human experience from which, especially in terms of intimacy, the official Church has drifted away. That is what inspired the recurring theme of the reflections of Pope John Paul II on "the person who acts."

Vatican II, then, is our ark, the collegial Church that understands that hierarchy went down with the *Upstairs/Downstairs* class divisions of the *Titanic* and that, as a people together, our calling is not less than healing the wounds in human personality. Our mission is to heal the Grail King, sexually wounded, groaning uneasily in his castle, that is the Institutional Church. We heal with the vision of Pope John XXIII, who wanted to offer the Church as pastoral servant to the world. First, however, the institution was to abandon the model of a triumphant monarchy sitting in lofty judgment on the lowly and pain-filled world. All it needs to do is ask the suffering world, full of regret about its past and anxious about its future, "What is it that ails you?"

VATICAN II AS SACRAMENT

We grasp John's commitment to a sacramental view of the world in his words at the very first session of the council in October 1962. Writing his address himself, or as he put it, "with meal from my own sack," he urged the Church to take "a turn away from a catastrophic reading of the situation of the Church and the world . . . a departure from the culture of fear and suspicion that has led to predominantly defensive choices in the government and life of the Church in order to isolate it and to protect its truth from the dangers of contamination to which encounter with others and the world could lead."[13]

John XXIII made an act of faith in the world and its bishops, "It pains us that we sometimes listen to the complaints of people who, though burning with zeal, are not endowed with an overabundance of discretion or measure. They see in modern times nothing but prevarication and ruin . . . as if in the time of the preceding ecumenical Councils everything represented a complete triumph for Christian ideas and for a rightful religious liberty. But we think we must disagree with these prophets of doom, who are always forecasting disaster, as though the end of the world were imminent."[14]

Defining the council's task more exactly, he said, "Our duty is not only to guard this precious treasure, as if we were only concerned with antiquity, but earnestly and fearlessly to dedicate ourselves to the work our age demands of us." The council, therefore, was not to express again teachings "well known and familiar to us all. For this a Council is not needed." The task, as John viewed it, was not to restate but to penetrate revelation more deeply: "The substance of the ancient doctrine of the deposit of the faith is one thing, and the way in which it is presented is another . . . while weighing everything in the forms and statements of a teaching activity that is predominantly pastoral in character. . . . Nowadays the Spouse of Christ prefers to use the medicine of mercy rather than severity. . . . She meets the needs of the present day more by demonstrating the validity of her teaching than by condemnation."[15]

JOHN'S SACRAMENTAL AND PASTORAL VISION

On the evening of the opening day of Vatican II, Pope John XXIII looked down from the window of his apartment at the huge and enthusiastic crowd gathered in the moonlit square below. Without a text, he addressed them as a pastor might his people. "Even the moon," he began, "may be said to have hastened on this evening. . . . When you return home you will find your children: Caress them and tell them: 'This is a caress from the Pope.' You will find some tears to dry. Speak words of comfort to the afflicted. Let the afflicted know that the Pope is with his sons and daughters, especially in hours of sadness and bitterness."[16] One cannot miss his pastoral commitment, in himself and the council, to healing in its deepest sense, identifying its medium as human relationships.

John sees a family before him and talks to it as a "brother" who is also a "father," saying, "It is a brother who speaks to you, a brother who, by the will of the Lord, has become a father. But fatherhood and brotherhood are both of them gifts of God. Everything is! Everything!"[17] John embraced all creation as a unity, without the exceptions and distinctions of those who continued to score deep divisions across the universe and human personality. His constant and confident theme was not fear of the world but sympathy for its suffering and his desire to bring healing to these wounds.

A few days later he addressed the non-Catholic observers whom he had invited to the council. He had, in fact, invited divided Christendom, in a variety of Protestant denominations and Orthodox and Oriental Churches, to constitute "the first collective meeting of non-Catholic representatives with the Pope of Rome."[18] Augustin Cardinal Bea, president of the Secretariat for Christian Unity, understood its innovative character, saying, "It's a miracle!"[19] The observers felt that they were taking on important roles in a transition in history.[20] But it is the address of the Pope himself that focuses on the long-open wound in the relationships of the Christian churches:

> Were you to read my heart, you would find there something more than finds expression in my words. How can I forget the ten years I spent in Sofia? And the ten years I spent in Istanbul and Athens? They were twenty happy, very useful years during which I came to know many venerable personages and young people full of generosity. I considered them my friends. . . . Later, in Paris, which is one of the crossroads of the world . . . I had many contacts with Christians belonging to various

denominations. Never, to my recollection, was there among
us muddling of principles, any disagreement at the level of
charity on the joint work which circumstances required of
us in aid of the suffering. We did not negotiate, we talked;
we did not debate but loved one another.[21]

The significance of this commitment to healing was indeed historic. "*For the first time* Christians of various Churches were no longer participants only in a purely bi-lateral dialogue, in which the emphasis on points of contact was matched by an emphasis, from others, on points of divergence: here they engaged in common exchange as equals [emphasis added]."[22]

John XXIII was intuitively sacramental in his view of the universe and immediately pastoral in his commitment to heal the terrible estrangements within Christianity itself. The council was, and remains, a dynamic event whose theme of healing, of treating the world as the Gospel Samaritan did the man who had been set upon by robbers on the road from Jerusalem to Jericho, giving him his mount, seeing that his wounds were treated and his lodging was secured. If the Church as Institution is capable of supporting and encouraging this pastoral sacramental approach to creation and creatures, it can draw on these sacred energies to heal the wound in human sexuality that it has so often exacerbated attitudes and actions that are countersacramental and counterpastoral.

HOPE FOR THE WOUNDED CHURCH

Therefore, the Church as Institution has within itself, perhaps forgotten or suppressed, the spiritual resources to examine and reform the divided model of creation and creatures that, in the name of what it terms a restoration, it is vigorously attempting to reinstate, enlarge, and maintain in its dealings with people. The pastoral, sacramental possibilities remain, however—and, indeed, live in the daily work of uncounted priests, religious and lay people who are active in the ministry of Catholic Christianity.

As we have seen, however, the present officials of the Church, whether they represent the mind of John Paul II or not, are determined to emphasize, as if these were the indispensable keys to the Kingdom, the division in humanity, between male and female, with the male ever in the superior, controlling role. They insist on a deep and clear-cut division in the personality between elements that are good, such as the intellect and the spirit, and those that are bad, such as the emotions and the flesh. So, too, sex is a furnace full of danger—touch, and be burned—instead of that central kindled source of warmth for the human family.

The sexual wounds of the institution are on display, not only in its anxious need to control the sexuality of the person rather than help the person to grow humanly and, therefore, sexually. The irritation and impatience of Church officials who rule out women as priests and emasculate men who marry rather than allow them to serve as priests, either, supporting these positions with theological and scriptural arguments that are inappropriate and inapplicable, betray their own sexual conflicts, the signs of which cannot be hidden and, indeed, are read, mostly with sympathy, by healthy people.

Only a terrible wound—that wound suffered in their very act of killing Nature—can explain how they can choose to diminish the availability of the sacraments to the world instead of enlarging the number of ministers who can celebrate them. To hold on so desperately to a principle that cannot be justified on any theological or scriptural basis is the evidence of defenses that, like the generals of World War I who did not understand the world in which they lived, allows them to sacrifice millions to their control of an old order that has already passed away. Great man that he is, Pope John Paul II, theoretically supportive of the unified person, maintains, to discomfort like that of the maimed Grail King, a divided model of human sexual functioning.

From around the world come reports almost every day of the

sexual problems of Catholic priests, of their inner lack of integration, of their finding themselves, to their own immense shame and pain, preying sexually on children placed in their care. The official Church will not make public any findings on the sexual problems of priests—often, for example, disgracing priests who have died from AIDS by changing their occupations and their final illness on the death certificates.

Perhaps the most obvious display of the unhealed wound in the Church as Institution is found in the attitudes and statements about homosexuality. It is described as against natural law, and homosexuals are said to harbor an intrinsic disorder. Yet while saying that, the Church accepts homosexual candidates for the priesthood, accepting what has been described as the evolution of "Lavender Rectories" and homosexual coteries in seminaries. Thus is their ambivalence toward homosexuality manifested as they allow to serve those on whom they also inflict pain. Yet most officials will not examine whether they have thereby become part of as primitive and unhealthy a sexual syndrome as we know.

WHAT WOULD HAPPEN IF . . . ?

Were the Church as Institution to take up again the pastoral self-examination that was and remains the work of Vatican II, what would occur? If this great and enormously influential body called for a true intermission, that coming "apart awhile" to which Jesus invited his apostles, in but this one area of its sexual teaching in order to explore it pastorally, what would the impact be on the Institution and on the world itself?

Healthy people throughout the Church would welcome and not be threatened by such a pause. Enormous tension would suddenly be eased for all believers because this intercession would be pastoral and, therefore, healing in itself. Great anxiety would, of course, enter the lives of the ecclesiastical bureaucrats who, as we have seen, answer their own obsessive emotional needs and preserve their jobs by maintaining the tension between abstract pronouncements on sexuality and the human experience of sexuality. They would oppose any interlude for pastoral reflection, no matter how positive or how clearly based on the latest scriptural and theological investigations. If this intermission would allow the Institution to catch up with itself theologically, it would send fear into the hearts of its worker bees whose careers depend on maintaining the time lag between intellectual advances and the organization's absorbing them fully into itself.

Excavating their riches does not mean that the Institution would sacrifice its teachings as—following the ancient Catholic dictum *fides quarens intellectum*, faith seeking to understand itself—it uncovers their radical, that is, *root*, meaning. The world would grow hushed and attend carefully, for every day beneath its supposed sexual sophistication, it feels the pain of its sexual woundedness. The racks of pornographic magazines, for example, are not the bold standards of Satan as much as they are the white flags of people worn out rather than renewed by the sexual revolution, people desperately and almost pitiably unsure of their sexual knowingness or personality integration.

Read only the Playboy Adviser to find that he deals in reassurance more than revolution. Are we surprised that GQ's counterpart counselor is named Dr. Sooth? Or that *Esquire* approached the millennium by publishing a medical school–like manual of the internal male organs to acquaint its allegedly worldly-wise readers with the biology of their own sexuality? Perhaps the sexual inhibitions of millions may best be read in the advertising in such magazines. Up front they may run cigarette ads that, like thirties movies, sell smoking as a masculine habit. In the back pages, one comes upon a picket line of defenses, each of them poignant in their testimony about underlying male shortcomings and inadequacies, from hair replacement to sexual-performance enhancement. Is this sinful or uncertain America? Are these tribunes of secure gender identity, or are they the sexually wounded wanting to get well?

Were the Institution, through its enormous pastoral capacity, to lower its voice and ask, "What is it that ails you?" would the response be one of relief or rebellion? The tension that now exists between the Institution and these countless numbers of humans struggling to understand and integrate their sexuality might not disappear, but it would lessen markedly. What would the Institution lose if, instead of issuing statements, such as those about the "objective disorder" of homosexuality, it sat, as a good pastor might, and willingly listened to the world and its sexual woes? The impulse of millions to set themselves against the authoritarianism of the Institution would be softened because the organization would be dropping its controlling stance so that the defensiveness it generates would be greatly reduced. What might the Church as Institution learn from the experience, confused and contradictory as it always emerges, of ordinary human beings who seek healing for their own sexual wounds? Healing, perhaps not with the completeness of a biblical miracle, but healing nonetheless, would follow in both the Institution and in the People who would know it now as a Mystery of understanding and reconciliation.

It is this Church as Institution, still able to draw on its pastoral health for wholeness, that must first examine its own extensive, untended, and long-denied sexual wound. It can find no place, in the Great Grail Castle Institution, where it may rest or find comfort. This official Church, so wounded in its illusory killing of Nature, longs for healing, but the court attendants remain silent for fear that they will violate institutional protocol. But in the world beyond, in the question the world would ask of itself about its wounded experience, the Institution would hear that inquiry and understand that it is directed at its own heart and begin its own healing and begin a new relationship to humankind.

What is it, what is it that ails you?

NOTES

✝

CHAPTER 1

1. Joseph Horowitz, "A New Tristan and Isolde in a Lustrous Lineage," *The New York Times*, November 21, 1999, Arts and Leisure, p. 1.

2. Ibid.

3. Joseph Campbell, *The Masks of God: Vol. IV, Creative Mythology* (New York: Viking, 1968), p. 224.

CHAPTER 3

1. Stephen R. Prescott, "White Robes and Crosses: Father John Conoley, the Ku Klux Klan, and the University of Florida," *Florida Historical Quarterly* 71, no. 1 (July 1992), p. 24.

2. Jennifer Egan, "Why a Priest," *The New York Times Magazine*, April 5, 1999.

3. Campbell, op. cit., p. 398.

CHAPTER 4

1. Wolfram von Eschenbach, *Parzival*, in *Wolfram von Eschenbach*, edited by Karl Lachman, 6th ed. (Leipzig: Walter de Gruyter & Co., 1926), Book IX, 47:8–16.

2. Campbell, op. cit., pp. 392, 393.

3. Op. cit., p. 452.

4. Gordon Allport, *The Individual and His Religion* (New York: Macmillan, 1950). See pp. 52 and 64 for his distinction between, and discussion of, immature religion, a social prop, and mature religion, a master motive in life.

5. Campbell, op. cit., p. 456.

6. Ibid.

7. Ibid.

CHAPTER 6

1. John L. McKenzie, *Dictionary of the Bible* (New York: Macmillan, 1965), p. 598.

CHAPTER 8

1. Gerald Kelly, S. J., *Modern Youth and Chastity* (St. Louis: The Queen's Work, 1941), p. 84. See also commentary by Leslie Griffin, "American Social Ethics," in *Moral Theology* 8, edited by Charles Curran and Richard McCormick, S. J. (Mahwah, N.J.: Paulist Press), pp. 453–485.
2. Griffin, op. cit., p. 457.
3. Ibid.
4. Op. cit., p. 462. Griffin notes that this was modified in a 1958 edition.
5. Kelly, op. cit., pp. 82, 84. Italics in original.

CHAPTER 9

1. Michael V. Gannon, "Before and After Modernism: The Intellectual Isolation of the American Priest," in *The Catholic Priest in the United States: Historical Investigations*, John Tracy Ellis, ed. (Washington, D.C.: USCC Publications, 1971), pp. 293–385.
2. Op. cit., p. 334.
3. Op. cit., p. 332.
4. Op. cit., p. 334.
5. Op. cit., p. 335.
6. Ibid.
7. Ibid.
8. Ibid.
9. Ibid.
10. Ibid.
11. Op. cit., p. 347.
12. Op. cit., p. 350.
13. Op. cit., p. 353.
14. Ibid.
15. Op. cit., p. 352. Gannon quotes from a 1923 issue of *Homiletic and Pastoral Review*, a popular magazine for Catholic clergy.
16. Op. cit., p. 354.
17. Op. cit., p. 355.

CHAPTER 10

1. Campbell, op. cit., p. 396.

2. Gannon, op. cit., p. 351.

3. Etienne Gilson, *History of Christian Philosophy in the Middle Ages* (New York: Random House, 1955), p. 45.

4. Summarized by Campbell, loc. cit.

5. Quoted from *Sic et Non*, in Campbell, p. 397.

6. See Gannon, loc. cit.

7. Ibid.

8. Quoted by Campbell, loc. cit., from *Historia Calamitatum*.

9. Ibid.

10. Ibid.

11. Op. cit., p. 398.

12. Michael Mott, *The Seven Mountains of Thomas Merton* (Boston: Houghton Mifflin, 1984), p. 411.

13. Op. cit., p. 438.

14. Quoted in Campbell, op. cit., p. 59, from Henry Osborn Taylor, *The Medieval Mind*, 4th ed. (Cambridge: Harvard University Press, 1925).

15. Op. cit., p. 60, from Taylor, pp. 42, 49.

16. Mott, op. cit., p. 450.

17. Op. cit., p. 533.

18. Op. cit., p. 564.

19. Op. cit., p. 565.

20. A. W. Richard Sipe, *Sex, Priests, and Power* (New York: Brunner/Mazel, 1995), p. 163.

21. Garry Wills, *Papal Sin* (New York: Doubleday, 2000), p. 88.

22. See Robert Blair Kaiser, *The Politics of Sex and Religion: A Case History in the Development of Doctrine* (Leaven Press of National Catholic Reporter, 1985) and Robert McClory, *The Turning Point: The Inside Story of the Papal Birth Control Commission* (New York: Crossroad, 1995).

23. Sipe, op. cit., p. 168.

24. Wills, loc. cit.

25. John Paul II, *The Role of the Christian Family in the Modern World* (Boston: Pauline Books, 1999), p. 48.

26. John Paul II, *The Theology of the Body, Human Love in the Divine Plan* (Boston: Pauline Books, 1997), p. 159.

27. Ibid.

CHAPTER 11

1. Ladislas M. Orsy, "Reception of Doctrine," in *Encyclopedia of Catholicism*, Richard McBrien, ed. (New York: HarperCollins, 1995), p. 1081.

2. Ibid.

3. Ibid.

4. Ibid.

5. Christopher O'Donnell, O. Carm., *Ecclesia, A Theological Encyclopedia of the Church* (Collegeville, Minn.: Liturgical Press, 1996), p. 400.

6. Ibid.

7. Op. cit., p. 401.

8. Ibid.

9. Ibid.

10. Ibid.

11. *Ordinatio Sacerdotalis* (Boston: Pauline Books, 1997), p. 7.

12. John L. Allen, Jr., *Cardinal Ratzinger* (New York, London: Continuum, 2000), pp. 185–87.

13. Ibid.

14. *Inter Insigniores*, presented in English as "On Admission of Women to the Priesthood" by Franjo Cardinal Seper, predecessor to Ratzinger as head of the Congregation of the Doctrine of the Faith, October 15, 1976.

15. Peter Hebblewaithe, *Paul VI, The First Modern Pope* (Mahwah, N.J.: Paulist Press, 1992), pp. 666 ff.

16. See Wills, *Papal Sin*, for an extensive review of this and associated arguments.

17. *Summa Theologica* 1, question 92, 1 *ad*1.

18. Op. cit., Supplement, question 39.

19. Again, see Wills, among others, for a detailed discussion.

20. Canon 813.1 (1984 Revision, Code of Canon Law).

21. Raymond Brown, *Biblical Reflections on Crises Facing the Church* (Mahwah, N.J.: Paulist Press, 1975), pp. 53, 54.

22. Ibid.

23. Uta Rank-Heinemann, *Eunuchs for the Kingdom of Heaven: Women, Sexuality, and the Catholic Church*, English edition (New York: Doubleday, 1990), pp. 126, 127.

24. Yves Congar, O. P., *Priest and Layman*, translated by P. J. Hepburne-Scott (London: Darton, Longman & Todd, 1996), pp. 74, 75.

CHAPTER 12

1. Hebblewaithe, op. cit., p. 442; see also Xavier Rynne, *Vatican Council II* (New York: Farrar, Strauss & Giroux, 1968), pp. 520, 521.

2. Rynne, loc. cit.

3. Interview with author, March 30, 1979.

4. *Sacerdotalis Caelibatus*, n. 88.

5. *The New Testament*, Confraternity Edition of the Holy Bible (New York: P. J. Kennedy), 1966.

6. John Paul II, *Letter to All Priests of the Church*, Holy Thursday, 1979, c. 8.

7. See Rank-Heinemann, op. cit., pp. 31–38, for an extended discussion of this and other transformations of New Testament writings on marriage that, thus distorted, have been used to justify celibacy for priests.

8. For a relevant discussion of popular and proper understandings of metaphor, see Jacques Barzun, *The American Scholar*, Autumn 1994, pp. 569 ff.

9. Tad Szulc, *Pope John Paul II: The Biography* (New York: Pocket Books, 1990), p. 41.

10. Op. cit., p. 66.

11. Joseph Campbell, *The Inner Reaches of Outer Space: Metaphor as Myth and as Religion* (New York: Alfred van Der Marck Editions, 1987), p. 60.

12. Op. cit., p. 59.

13. See Kennedy and Heckler, op. cit.; also, Sipe, op. cit.

14. Donald Cozzens, *The Changing Face of the Priesthood* (Collegeville, Minn.: Liturgical Press, 2000), pp. 97–103.

15. Kennedy and Heckler, op. cit.

16. William C. Holmes, M.S.C.E., and Gail B. Slap, M.D., M.S., "Sexual Abuse of Boys: Definition, Prevalence, Correlates, Sequelae, and Management," *Journal of the American Medical Association*, December 2, 1998, p. 1858.

17. *Policies and Procedures of the Archdiocese of Chicago for Addressing Accusations of Child Abuse*, Archdiocese of Chicago, 1989.

18. For a thoughtful analysis, see Sipe, op. cit., especially Part Two, "Function and Failure."

CHAPTER 13

1. Canon 277. 1.

2. Archbishop J. Francis Stafford, "Eucharistic Foundations of Sacerdotal Celibacy," *Origins* 23, no. 12 (September 2, 1993). A paper delivered by the now Cardinal Stafford at a conference at the Gregorian University in Rome, sponsored by the Vatican Congregation of the Clergy, May 26–28, 1993.

3. Franz Josef von Beeck, citing Southern's *Western Society and the Church of the Middle Ages*, in "The Women in My Life," *Commonweal*, January 29, 1999, p. 16.

4. Barbara Susan Balboni, "A Descriptive Study of the American Catholic Bishops' Understanding of Clergy Sexual Molestation and Abuse of Children and Adolescents," Ph.D. Dissertation, Northeastern University, Boston, Mass., 1998, p. 18.

5. Jimmy Breslin, *World Without End, Amen* (New York: The Viking Press, 1972). Throughout the novel, the author shows how the selective perception of some police allowed them to construct a protective, denial-filled world even when they suffered disciplinary action.

6. Laurie Goodstein, "Egan Faces Test in Role of Shepherd and C.E.O.," *The New York Times*, Metropolitan Desk, June 18, 2000, p. 1.

7. Cozzens, op. cit., p. 100.

8. Op. cit., pp. 101, 102.

9. Op. cit., p. 185.

10. Jennifer Egan, op. cit., p. 33.

11. Sister Katarina Schuth, *Seminaries, Theologates and the Future of Church Ministry* (Collegeville, Minn.: Liturgical Press, 1999), p. 228.

12. Egan, op. cit., pp. 31, 32.

13. Ibid.

14. Ibid.

15. Ibid.

16. Ibid.

17. Ibid.

18. Egan, op. cit., p. 49.

19. Op. cit., p. 55.

20. Pamela Schaeffer, "Gramick Says No to Vatican Silencing, Expects Dismissal," *National Catholic Reporter*, June 16, 2000, p. 4.

21. Excerpted in *Our Sunday Visitor*, July 25, 1999, p. 3.

22. Ibid.

23. Tom Roberts, "Gramick on Conscience in Lincoln," *National Catholic Reporter*, May 5, 2000, p. 6.

24. Ibid.

25. Teresa Malcolm, "Letter Ends Parishioners' Two Decades of Service," *National Catholic Reporter*, November 5, 1999, p. 3.

26. Associated Press, "Priests Dying of AIDS at High Rate, Report Says," January 29, 2000.

27. Interview with author, May 13, 2000.

28. Ibid.

29. Ibid.

CHAPTER 14

1. Robert McClory, "Bishops Ponder New Study of Priest Shortage," *National Catholic Reporter*, June 30, 2000, p. 5.

2. Ibid.

3. Ibid.
4. Ibid.
5. See Cozzens, loc. cit.
6. Rudolph Bell and Donald Weinstein, *Saints and Society* (Chicago: University of Chicago Press, 1982).
7. Op. cit., p. 189.
8. Ibid.
9. Rudolph Bell, *Holy Anorexia* (Chicago: University of Chicago Press, 1985).
10. Op. cit., p. 151.
11. Op. cit., p. 150.

CHAPTER 15

1. *The Barnhart Concise Dictionary of Etymology*, Robert Barnhart, ed. (New York: HarperCollins, 1995), p. 357.
2. Francis Cardinal George, Archbishop of Chicago, in remarks at the Commonweal Symposium, Loyola University, Chicago, Ill., October 6, 1999.
3. *Caudium et Spes*, Pastoral Constitution on the Church in the Modern World, the principal pastoral document of Vatican II, n. 9.
4. Op. cit., n. 11.
5. "For Lost Pregnancies, New Rites of Mourning," *The New York Times*, January 25, 1998, p. 1.
6. Presidential address, Division of Psychology and Religion, American Psychological Association, August 17, 1997.
7. Ibid.
8. *HarperCollins Encyclopedia of Catholicism*, Richard McBrien, ed. (New York: HarperCollins, 1995), p. 471.
9. John L. Allen, Jr., "Structure Meant Survival Study Finds," *National Catholic Reporter*, October 8, 1999, p. 12.
10. Ibid.
11. Ibid.
12. Campbell, op. cit., p. 4.
13. *History of Vatican II*, vol. 2, eds. Giussepe Alberigo and Joseph Komanchak (Maryknoll, N.Y.: Orbis, 1997), p. 15.
14. Ibid.
15. Ibid.
16. Op. cit., p. 20.
17. Ibid.
18. Op. cit., p. 22.

19. Op. cit., p. 23.
20. Ibid.
21. Ibid.
22. Ibid.